Numeracy Pupil's Book
Year 3

Peter Patilla &
Paul Broadbent

EDUCATIONAL

Every effort has been made to trace copyright holders and to obtain their permission for the use of copyright material. The authors and publishers will gladly receive information enabling them to rectify any error or omission in subsequent editions.

First published 1999,Reprinted 1999, 2001, 2002

Letts Educational, The Chiswick Centre, 414 Chiswick High Road, London,W4 5TF
Tel: (020) 8996 3333
Fax: (020) 8742 8390

Text © Peter Patilla and Paul Broadbent
Editorial, design and production © Gecko Limited, Bicester, Oxon
Illustrations © Peter and Janet Simmonett, except Beccy Blake: pp. 10, 42; Michael Brownlow: p. 72; Jan Nesbitt: p. 28; Jake Tebbit: pp. 14, 30; Andy Warrington: pp. 16, 74, additional graphics: Claire-Louise Simmonett. Cover illustration © Beccy Blake.

British Library Cataloguing-in-Publication Data
A CIP record for this book is available from the British Library.

ISBN 1 84085 273 9
Printed in the UK by Scotprint
Letts Educational is part of the Granada Learning Group. Granada Learning is a division of Granada plc.

CONTENTS

Do you remember?

1 **What is the next number in the sequence?**

   a 16   **b** 17   **c** 18

11	13	15	☐

2 **What is this number?**

   a 74   **b** 704   **c** 47

seventy-four

3 **What is the answer?**

   a 506   **b** 56   **c** 110

50 + 6

4 **What is a half of the set?**

   a 2   **b** 3   **c** 4

5 **What is the missing number?**

   a 10   **b** 11   **c** 12

$$\square - 1 = 11$$

6 **What is the total?**

a £1.15   **b** £2.15   **c** 17p

---

7 **What is the missing number?**

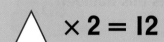

$$\triangle \times 2 = 12$$

a 6   **b** 10   **c** 14

---

8 **What is the time?**

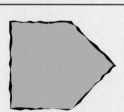

a 6.45   **b** 7.15   **c** 9.30

---

9 **What is this shape?**

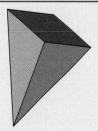

a square   **b** rectangle   **c** pentagon

---

10 **What is this shape?**

a pyramid   **b** square   **c** cone

Check your answers on page 96.

Place value

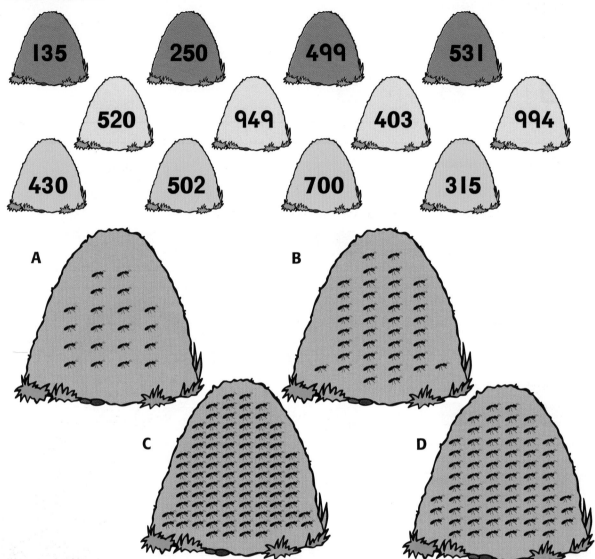

1 Write the numbers on the orange hills in words.

2 Write the numbers on the yellow hills in order.

3 Write one less than the numbers on the green hills.

4 There are 20 ants in ant hill A.

Estimate how many ants there are in:

ant hill B

ant hill C

ant hill D.

Practice

A Write the missing numbers.

I 346 = 300 + 40 + ☐

2 219 = 200 + ☐ + 9

3 520 = ☐ + 20 + 0

4 607 = ☐ + ☐ + 7

5 815 = ☐ + 10 + ☐

6 350 = ☐ + 50 + ☐

7 475 = 400 + ☐ + ☐

8 829 = ☐ + ☐ + 9

B Where does each arrow point? Write the number.

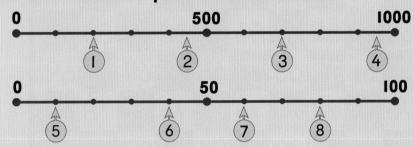

C What does each reading show?

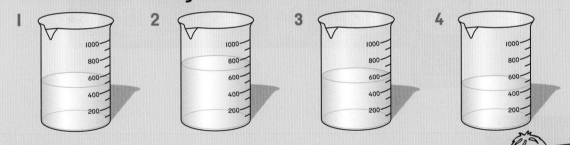

Challenge

Words of the week

digits

tens

hundreds

Arrange these digits to make 3-digit numbers.

How many can you find?

Write them in order.

Addition and subtraction

0	1	2	3	4	5	6	7	8	9
10	11	12	13	14	15	16	17	18	19
20	21	22	23	24	25	26	27	28	29
30	31	32	33	34	35	36	37	38	39
40	41	42	43	44	45	46	47	48	49
50	51	52	53	54	55	56	57	58	59
60	61	62	63	64	65	66	67	68	69
70	71	72	73	74	75	76	77	78	79
80	81	82	83	84	85	86	87	88	89
90	91	92	93	94	95	96	97	98	99
100									

Starters

Only use multiples of 5.

$$\square + \triangle = 100 \qquad \square + \triangle + \bigcirc = 100$$

1 What if both numbers must be odd?

2 What if both numbers must be even?

3 What if the numbers must be equal?

4 What if the $\square$ number is 50?

5 What if the $\triangle$ number is 5?

6 What if the $\bigcirc$ number is 25?

Practice

A Total each set of numbers.

| 1 | 36 | 5 | | 2 | 7 | 53 | | 3 | 9 | 66 |

1 36 5   2 7 53   3 9 66

4 48 8   5 7 43 20   6 25 9 21

7 50 6 34   8 8 50 42   9 40 30 20

10 50 10 80   11 60 80 20   12 50 50 50

B Copy and complete the tables.

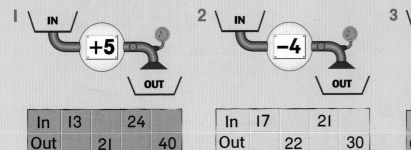

1 IN **+5** OUT

In	13		24	
Out		21		40

2 IN **−4** OUT

In	17		21	
Out		22		30

3 IN **+9** OUT

In	7		15	
Out		12		22

C 1 36 plus 20.

2 75 minus 25.

3 Total 15 and 23.

4 Subtract 35 from 100.

5 What must be added to 23 to make 100?

6 What is the difference between 15 and 70?

7 What is the sum of 15, 20 and 14?

8 What is double 17?

Challenge

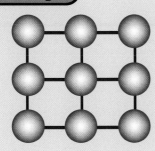

Put the numbers 1 to 9 in the circles.

Joined numbers must have an odd difference.

Words of the week

total

calculate

plus

minus

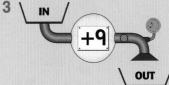

Money and problems

Smith's ices
Small cornet 40p
Large cornet 99p
Wafer 40p
Choc ice £1.25
Tub 50p
Lolly tube 55p
Zoom bar 45p
Drink on a stick 75p

Luigi's ices
Zoom bar 40p
Lolly tube 65p
Tub 60p
Choc ice £1
Small cornet 45p
Large cornet 90p
Wafer 40p
Drink on a stick 80p

Starters

1 Who sells the dearest choc ices?

2 What would two large cornets from Smith's cost?

3 What would a lolly tube and a small cornet cost from Luigi?

4 How much change from £1 would Luigi give for a wafer?

5 I want a lolly tube and a Zoom bar.
   How much cheaper are Smith's than Luigi's?

6 What would you buy for £2?
   Write a list.

Practice

A Write the totals.

1 £1 50p 5p   2 £2 5p 1p   3 £1 10p 2p

4 £2 £1 20p   5 £2 1p 1p   6 £2 £2 50p

7 £1 £1 1p   8 £2 50p 20p   9 £1 20p 2p

B Write the change from £5.

1 £3.50 ◎   2 £1.25 ◎   3 £4.60 ◎   4 £2.20 ◎   5 50p ◎

C Look at the bills.

Write the change from £10.

1

book	£2.50
magazine	£2.00
disc	£3.50

2

cola	80p
squash	70p
lime	60p

3

Blaster	£1.50
Zoom	£2.20
Flash	£1.10

D

1 £1.60 ◎

What would 2 cost?
How much change from £5?

2 £2.50 ◎

What would 3 cost?
How much change from £10?

3 £1.10 ◎

What would 5 cost?
How much change from £10?

4 £2.80 ◎

What would 2 cost?
How much change from £10?

Words of the week

note
expensive
amount
value

Challenge

You have £5.

Which three books could you buy?

Space
Football £1.60
Plants
Dogs £1.20
Horses
Pop
£2.50
£1.80
£2.30
£1.50

Measures

A

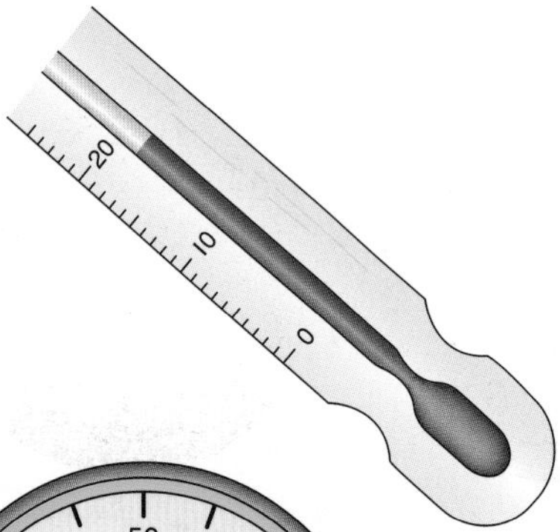

B

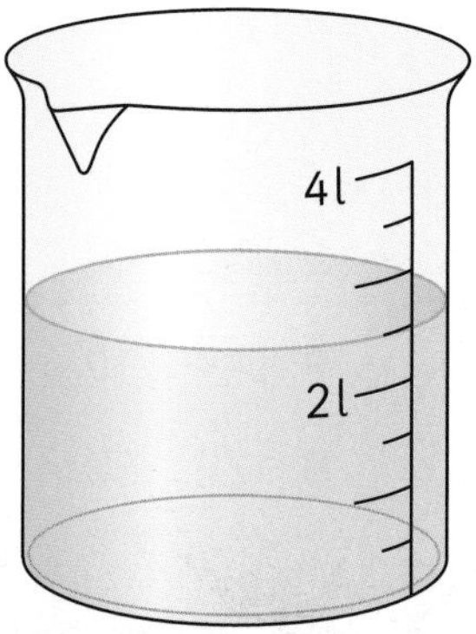

4l

2l

C

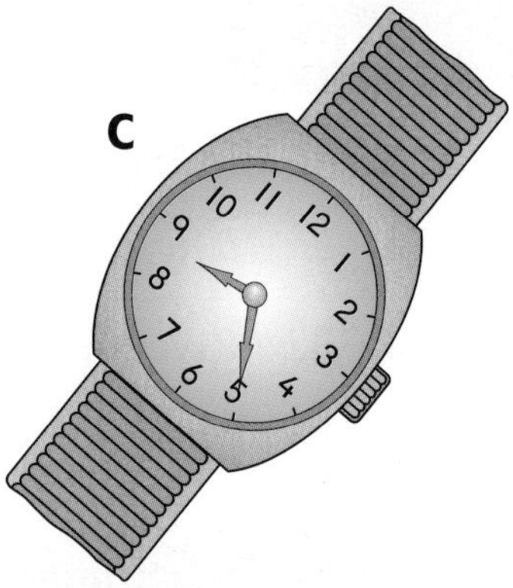

D

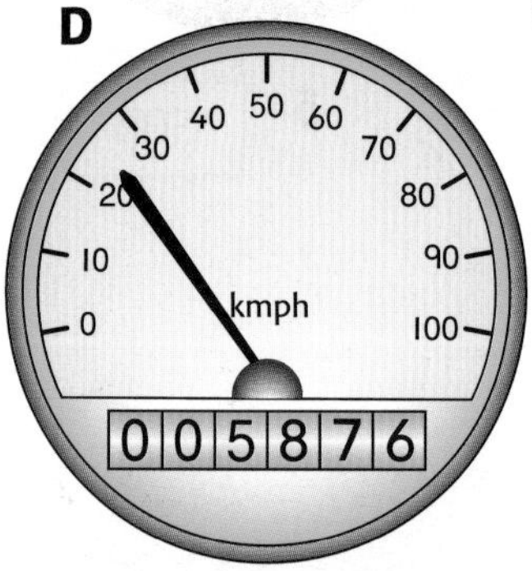

kmph

0 0 5 8 7 6

E

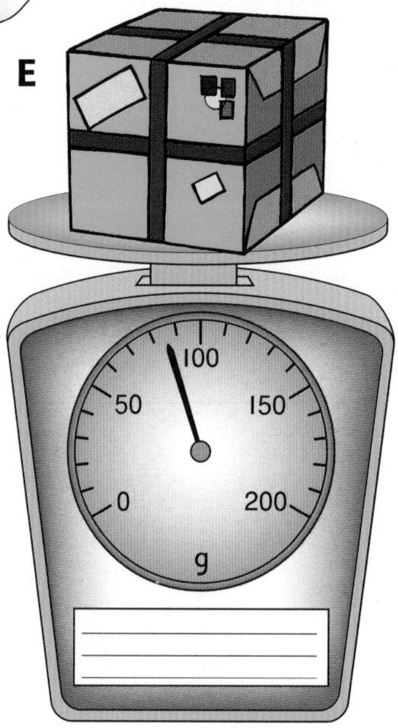

100

50   150

0   200

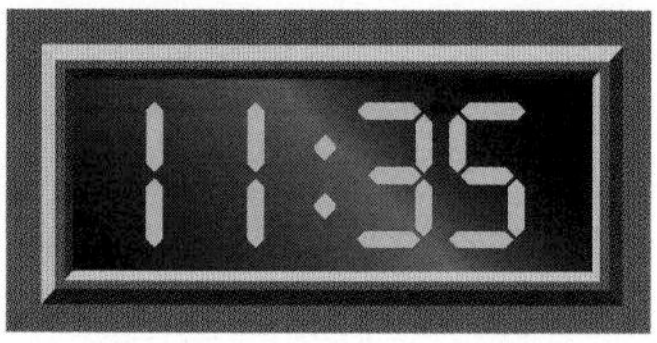

g

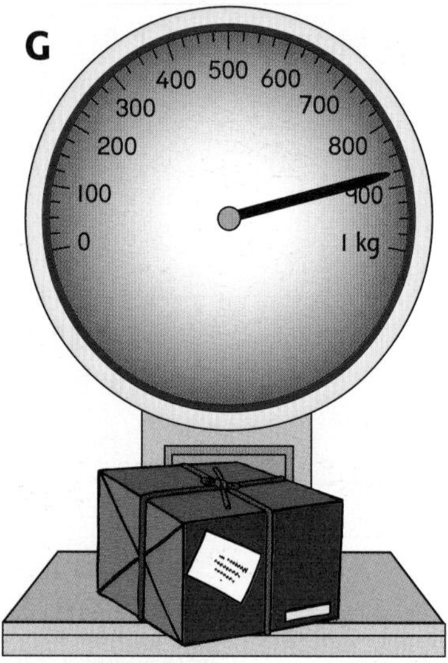

F

11:35

G

400 500 600
300   700
200   800
100   900
0   1 kg

I

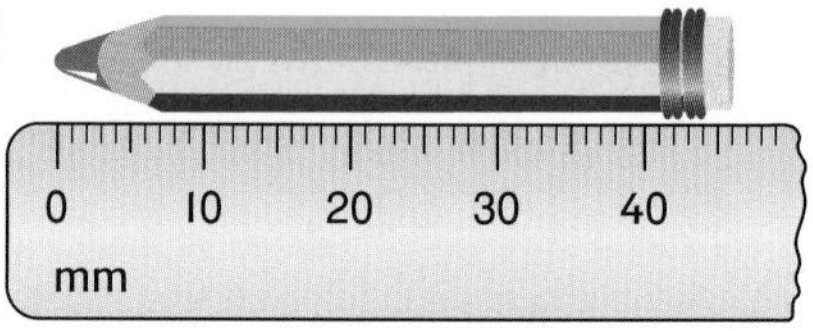

0   10   20   30   40

mm

H

cm 1   2   3   4   5   7

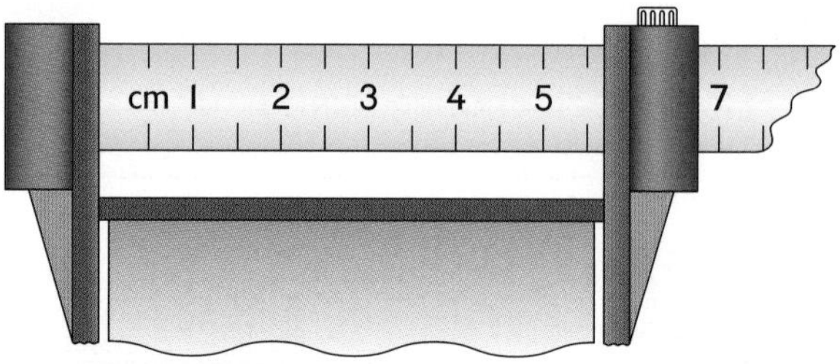

Starters

1 About how long is the pencil?
3 How fast is the car going?
5 How heavy is each parcel?

2 What do the times say?
4 What is the temperature?

Practice

A Write the times.

1
2
3
4

B Write the time one hour later.

1
2
3
4

C Which units would you use?

1   The distance to Paris
2   The height of a door
3   The capacity of a bath
4   The length of a pencil
5   Your weight
6   The weight of a spoon

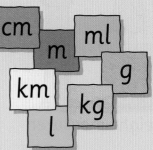

D I think of a length, double it and add 5 cm.

The new length is 45 cm.

Which length did I think of?

Words of the week
approximately
division
kilometre

Challenge

Which measuring words can you find beginning with –

centi ...   **deci ...**   **kilo ...**

Length

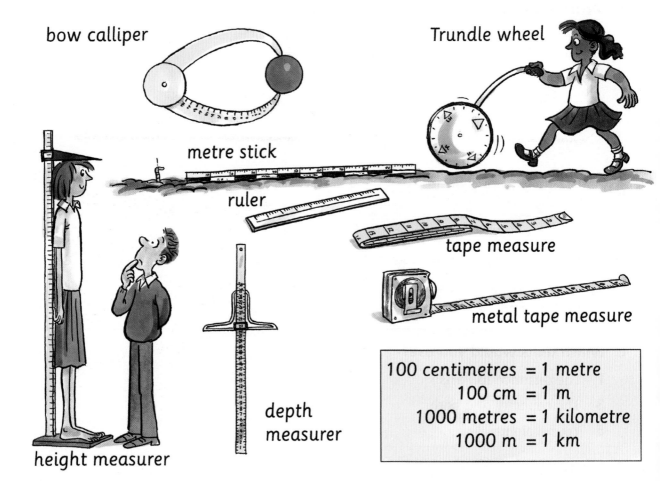

bow calliper

Trundle wheel

metre stick

ruler

tape measure

metal tape measure

depth measurer

height measurer

100 centimetres = 1 metre
100 cm = 1 m
1000 metres = 1 kilometre
1000 m = 1 km

Starters

What instrument would you use to measure these?

1 the length of the playground
2 how tall you are
3 round your waist
4 how deep a bottle is
5 across a bottle
6 height of a desk
7 width of this book
8 height of a door

Practice

A Measure these lines to the nearest half cm.

1 ──────────── 2 ────────────────

3 ──────── 4 ───────

5 ─────────── 6 ────────────

7 ───── 8 ──────────────

B 1 A 2 metre plank has 45 cm cut off it.
How much is left?

2 Two ribbons are 25 cm and 51 cm long.
What is the difference in their lengths?

3 A 5 metre roll of tape has $1\frac{1}{2}$ metres cut off.
How much is left on the roll?

4 Lou is 1.2 m tall, Sam is 1 metre tall.
How much taller is Lou than Sam?

5 A 3 metre length of wool is cut in half.
How long is each piece?

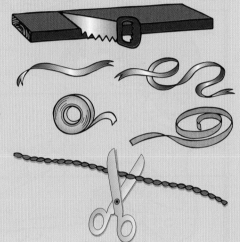

C 1 3.2 m = ☐ m + ☐ cm **2** 150 cm = 1.☐ m **3** 1.25 m = ☐ cm

  1.5 m = ☐ m + ☐ cm   225 cm = 2.☐ m   4.75 m = ☐ cm

  4.5 m = ☐ m + ☐ cm   275 cm = 2.☐ m   3.5 m = ☐ cm

  2.6 m = ☐ m + ☐ cm   300 cm = 3.☐ m   4.5 m = ☐ cm

Challenge

**Find out the circumference and perimeter
of different objects.**

Estimate first, then measure.

Make a table of results.

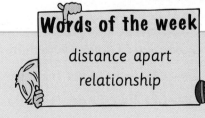

Words of the week

distance apart
relationship

Shape and space

Starters

1 What is four squares E of the hut?

2 What is three squares N of the tree?

3 What is two squares W then two squares S of the skull?

4 Describe how to get from the cave to the volcano.

5 Describe how to get from the wreck to the bridge.

Practice

A Draw a table like this:

All right angles	Some right angles	No right angles

Draw round some shapes in each part of the table.

B Name and describe each shape.

1 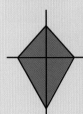 2   3   4   5   6

C Look at the shapes above.

Write their names in a table like this one:

prisms	
not prisms	

D Draw round some quadrilaterals.

Name and describe each one.
Draw in lines of symmetry.

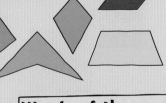

names	special things
rectangle	2 lines of symmetry
diamond	4 sides the same
rhombus	

Words of the week
quadrilaterals
right angles
prism
hemisphere

Challenge

Choose three different triangles.

Make a symmetrical
pattern using these shapes.

17

Review

A How much are the red digits worth?

1   **425**   2   **205**   3   **479**   4   **936**

B Which numbers do the arrows point to?

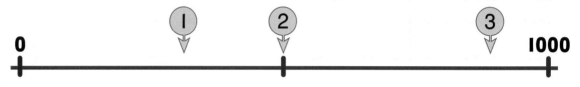

0   1000

C 1   15 + 6 = ☐   2   ☐ + 5 = 24   3   13 + ☐ = 22

4   20 − 3 = ☐   5   ☐ − 4 = 17   6   23 − ☐ = 13

D Write the totals.

1   30p 80p   2   75p 50p   3   40p 50p 80p

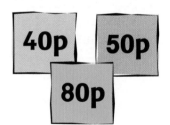

E Write the change from £5.

1   **60p**   2   **£1.50**   3   **£3.50**   4   **£2.70**

F **Write the times.**

1

2

3

4

G **Measure each line to the nearest cm.**

1 ▬▬▬▬▬▬▬▬▬▬▬

2 ▬▬▬▬▬▬▬

3 ▬▬▬▬▬▬▬▬▬▬▬▬

4 ▬▬▬▬▬▬▬▬▬▬

H 1 3 metres 20 cm = ⬜ cm

2 1 metre 5 cm = ⬜ cm

3 2 metres 25 cm = ⬜ cm

4 5 metres 75 cm = ⬜ cm

I **Name each shape.**

1

2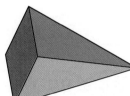

3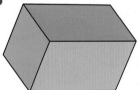

4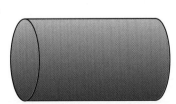

5

J **Draw three different quadrilaterals.**

Each quadrilateral must have a right angle.

Counting

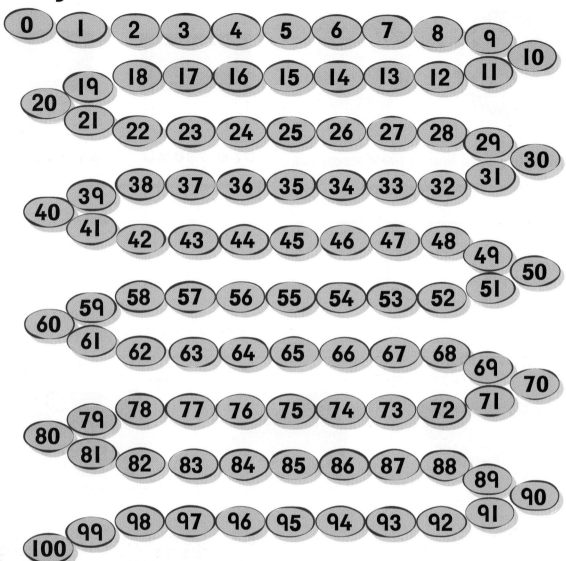

Starters

1 Write all the odd numbers between 50 and 60.
2 Write all the even numbers between 70 and 90.
3 Write all the multiples of 5 between 35 and 75.
4 Write all the odd multiples of 3 between 10 and 30.
5 Write all the even multiples of 3 between 90 and 100.

Practice

A tens ones

How many in each set?

B Write the missing numbers.

1	3	13	23	33		
2	96	86	76	66		
3	105	115	125	135		
4	396	386	376	366		

C These are '2 more than' chains. Write the missing numbers.

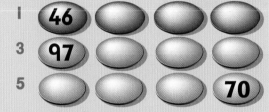

1 **46** ◯ ◯ ◯

2 **71** ◯ ◯ ◯

3 **97** ◯ ◯ ◯

4 ◯ ◯ ◯ **99**

5 ◯ ◯ ◯ **70**

6 ◯ ◯ ◯ **56**

D Copy the diagram.

Write these numbers on the diagram.

odd numbers | multiples of 3

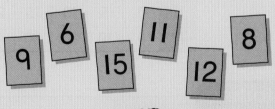

9 6 15 11 12 8

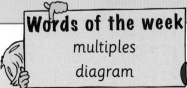

Challenge

Two odd numbers always add up to an even number. → Is this TRUE or NOT TRUE?

Multiplication tables

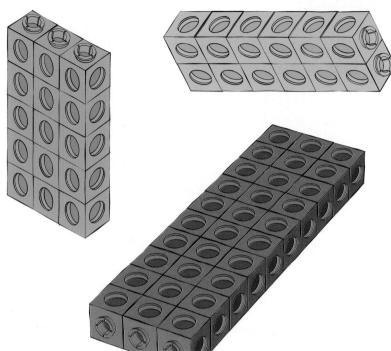
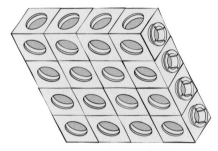

×	0	1	2	3	4	5	6	7	8	9	10
2	0	2	4	6	8	10	12	14	16	18	20
3	0	3	6	9	12	15	18	21	24	27	30
4	0	4	8	12	16	20	24	28	32	36	40
5	0	5	10	15	20	25	30	35	40	45	50
10	0	10	20	30	40	50	60	70	80	90	100

Starters

1 Write a multiplication fact for each array of cubes.
2 Twice as many red cubes: how many is this?
3 Half as many blue cubes: how many is this?
4 Three times as many pink cubes: how many is this?
5 Which arrays will total 36 cubes?

Practice

A **1** $5 \times 2 =$ ☐

   $4 \times 4 =$ ☐

   $3 \times 5 =$ ☐

   $10 \times 3 =$ ☐

   $9 \times 5 =$ ☐

2 $10 \times$ ☐ $= 40$

   $3 \times$ ☐ $= 27$

   $4 \times$ ☐ $= 12$

   $5 \times$ ☐ $= 35$

   $2 \times$ ☐ $= 18$

3 ☐ $\times 1 = 5$

   ☐ $\times 2 = 20$

   ☐ $\times 4 = 24$

   ☐ $\times 5 = 45$

   ☐ $\times 3 = 9$

B **1** $16 \div 2 =$ ☐

   $40 \div 10 =$ ☐

   $9 \div 3 =$ ☐

   $35 \div 5 =$ ☐

   $50 \div 5 =$ ☐

2 $30 \div$ ☐ $= 6$

   $45 \div$ ☐ $= 9$

   $16 \div$ ☐ $= 8$

   $25 \div$ ☐ $= 5$

   $90 \div$ ☐ $= 9$

3 ☐ $\div 2 = 5$

   ☐ $\div 5 = 6$

   ☐ $\div 10 = 7$

   ☐ $\div 3 = 5$

   ☐ $\div 4 = 8$

C **1** Double 7

   2 3 times 4

   3 Multiply 10 by 6

   4 9 multiplied by 2

   5 Three fives

   6 Halve 18

   7 How many 5s in 35?

   8 Divide 15 by 3

   9 Share 16 by 4

   10 24 divided by 4

D **1** Joe buys five 7p stamps.
   How much is this?

   2 Alex has £5.
   Fran has four times as much.
   How much has Fran?

   3 Nigel has 24 shells.
   He puts 4 shells in every tin.
   How many tins does he need?

   4 Vineeta has £20 in £2 coins.
   How many coins has she?

Challenge

Find several answers for each problem:

☐ $\times$ △ $= 60$ ☐ $\div$ △ $= 3$

Words of the week

product

array

row

column

Multiplication problems

Gloves	£3 a pair
Hats	£5
Scarves	£4
Socks	£2 a pair
T-shirts	£6
Shorts	£9

Starters

1 What would 3 pairs of gloves cost?

2 What would 6 pairs of socks cost?

3 What would 4 hats cost?

4 How many hats can be bought for £20?

5 How many T-shirts can be bought for £20?

Practice

A Multiply each set of numbers together.

1 (2) (3) (5)   2 (3) (4) (2)   3 (4) (2) (5)   4 (4) (5) (3)

B Multiply each number by 10.

1	9	2	11	3	19	4	24	5	29	6	30
7	36	8	75	9	91	10	59	11	41	12	50
13	73	14	46	15	87	16	99

C

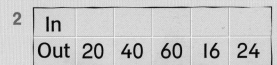

Copy and fill in the tables.

1

In	4	6	7	8	10
Out					

2

In					
Out	20	40	60	16	24

D Double each number.

1 (12)   2 (22)   3 (15)   4 (30)

5 (80)   6 (60)   7 (50)   8 (90)

Words of the week

multiply
divide
double
halve

Challenge

Look at the sets of numbers.

4   6   24

3   9   27

Write multiplication and division sums with each set.

25

Fractions

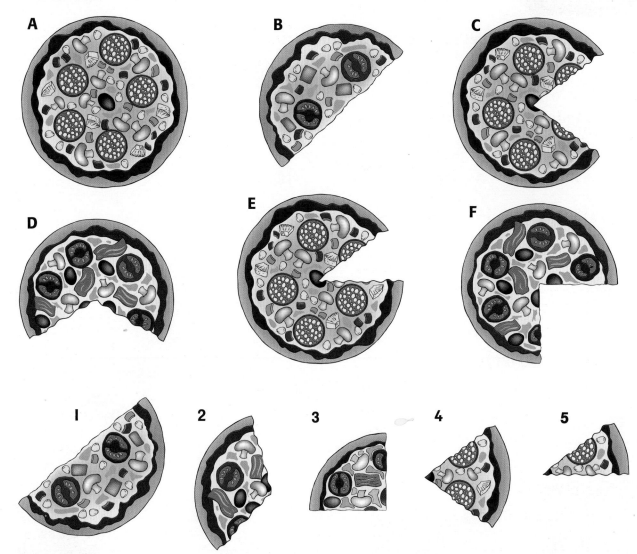

Starters

1 Which pizza has the biggest slice missing?

2 Which pizza has the smallest slice missing?

3 Which pizza has one third missing?

4 Which pizza has one quarter missing?

5 Which pizza has one fifth missing?

Can you find where each slice fits?

Practice

A **What fraction of each set of balloons is ringed?**

1

2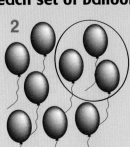

3

4

B 1 Find $\frac{1}{2}$ of these.

8
12
18
24
30

2 Find $\frac{1}{10}$ of these.

20
50
70
90
100

3 Find $\frac{1}{5}$ of these.

10
20
15
25
45

4 Find $\frac{1}{4}$ of these.

8
16
20
32
40

C **What is $\frac{1}{2}$ of these?**

1 (7)   2 (9)   3 (13)   4 (19)

5 (£3)   6 (£5)   7 (£9)   8 (£11)

Challenge

Make a shape from 20 cubes.

The shape must be red, white and blue:
$\frac{1}{2}$ red, $\frac{1}{10}$ blue, and the rest white.

Words of the week

fraction
halve
half

Subtraction and time

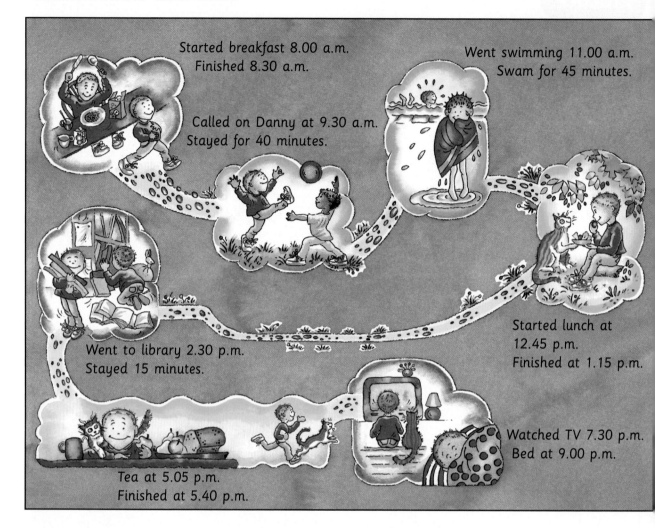

Started breakfast 8.00 a.m.
Finished 8.30 a.m.

Went swimming 11.00 a.m.
Swam for 45 minutes.

Called on Danny at 9.30 a.m.
Stayed for 40 minutes.

Started lunch at 12.45 p.m.
Finished at 1.15 p.m.

Went to library 2.30 p.m.
Stayed 15 minutes.

Watched TV 7.30 p.m.
Bed at 9.00 p.m.

Tea at 5.05 p.m.
Finished at 5.40 p.m.

Starters

Look at the diagram of Sam's day.

1 How long was breakfast?

2 What time did Sam leave Danny's?

3 When was swimming over?

4 How long was lunch?

5 What time did Sam leave the library?

6 How long did tea take?

7 How long did Sam watch TV?

8 How long was Sam's day?

Practice

A

1  **+ 30**

In				
Out	50	64	95	100

2 **− 12**

In				
Out	0	12	20	54

3 **+ 22**

In				
Out	22	26	52	95

B Copy and write in the missing numbers.

1
24 + 37 = 61

61 − 37 = ☐

61 − 24 = ☐

2
82 − 57 = 25

57 + 25 = ☐

82 − 25 = ☐

3
73 − 49 = 24

73 − 24 = ☐

24 + 49 = ☐

C Write the differences between these pairs.

1 48 53   **2** 75 84   **3** 123 130   **4** 218 225   **5** 342 337

D

1 How much more than 50 is the total of 13 and 46?

2 How much less than 50 is the difference between 60 and 54?

3 What must be added to 50 to make the answer to 7 × 10?

4 What must be subtracted from 50 to make the answer to 2 × 9?

5 What was added to 50 to make 99?

Words of the week
difference
a.m.
p.m.

Challenge

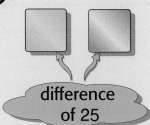

difference of 25

What could the two numbers be?

Find six solutions.

Graphs

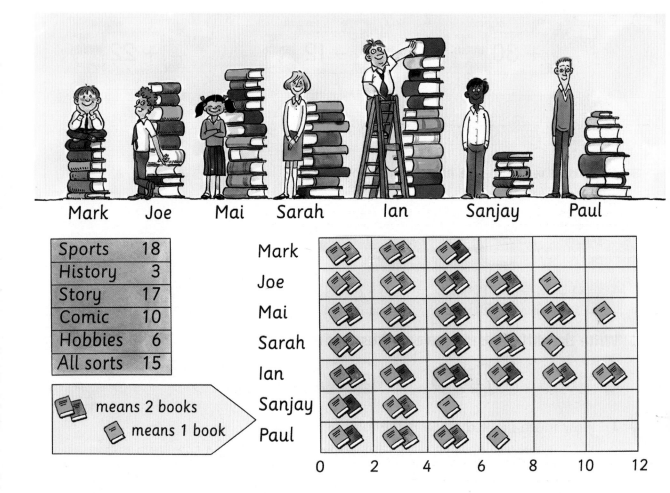

Sports	18
History	3
Story	17
Comic	10
Hobbies	6
All sorts	15

means 2 books
means 1 book

Starters

1 How many books did Mai read?
2 Who read 9 books?
3 Who read more than 10 books?
4 How many of the books were about hobbies?
5 Who read most books?

Practice

A Jelly babies

Red	🍬🍬🍬🍬🍬🍬🍬
Yellow	🍬🍬🍬
Green	🍬🍬🍬🍬🍬
Purple	🍬🍬
Orange	🍬🍬🍬🍬🍬🍬🍬
Pink	🍬🍬🍬🍬

 = 2 jelly babies

= 1 jelly baby

1 Which is the most common colour?

2 Which is the least common colour?

3 How many yellow jelly babies are there?

4 How many green jelly babies are there?

5 How many more orange jelly babies are there than pink ones?

B Vote on favourite colours in your class.

Draw a table to show what you find.

Favourite	Votes
Red	
Yellow	

Words of the week

diagram

chart

graph

Challenge

Collect information about hair colour and eye colour.

Draw a graph to show your information.

Review

A Name three odd numbers between 51 and 81.

51 — ☐ — ☐ — ☐ — 81

B Name three even numbers between 80 and 100.

80 — ☐ — ☐ — ☐ — 100

C $2 \times 9 = \triangle$ $5 \times 9 = \triangle$ $7 \times 2 = \triangle$

D $25 \div \triangle = 5$ $12 \div \triangle = 6$ $15 \div \triangle = 3$

E $\square \times 6 = 12$ $\square \times 5 = 50$ $\square \times 4 = 0$

F $12 \div 3 = \square$ $60 \div 10 = \square$ $45 \div 5 = \square$

G Double each number.

| 10 | 12 | 15 | 25 | 40 | 35 |

H Halve each number.

| 40 | 30 | 5 | 9 | 17 | 24 |

I   Which are thirds?

1 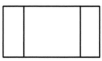   2   3 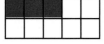   4

J   What is the coloured fraction?

1 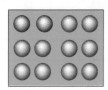   2   3   4

K   What fraction of the spots are coloured red?

1 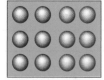   2 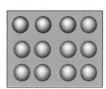   3 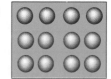   4

L 1

$26 + 48 = 74$

$74 - 48 =$ ▢

$74 - 26 =$ ▢

2

$91 - 72 = 19$

$72 + 19 =$ ▢

$91 - 19 =$ ▢

3

$52 - 18 = 34$

$52 - 34 =$ ▢

$34 + 18 =$ ▢

M   What is 40 minutes after **?**

N   How many minutes between **and** **?**

O   Multiply each number by 10.

15   30   75   46   71

Do you remember?

1 What does the number say?

406

a forty six   **b** four hundred and six   **c** four hundred and sixty

2 Where is the arrow pointing?

0   1000

a 40   **b** 400   **c** 600

3 What is the total?

a £25   **b** £2.50   **c** £2.05

4 How much is in the jug?

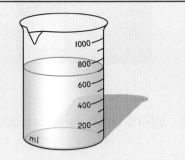

a 500 ml   **b** 650 ml   **c** 700 ml

5 What is the same as 120 cm?

a 1.2 m   **b** 12 m   **c** 1.2 km

6 **What is the missing number?**

$$\boxed{} + 40 = 100$$

a 60   **b** 50   **c** 40

---

7 **What is the shape called?**

a circle   **b** hemisphere   **c** prism

---

8 **What is the shape called?**

a quadrilateral   **b** pentagon   **c** hexagon

---

9 **Is the angle a right angle?**

a Yes   **b** No

---

10 **What is the missing number?**

$$\boxed{} \times 5 = 45$$

a 5   **b** 7   **c** 9

Check your answers on page 96. ✓

Place value

Use beads or counters on this abacus.

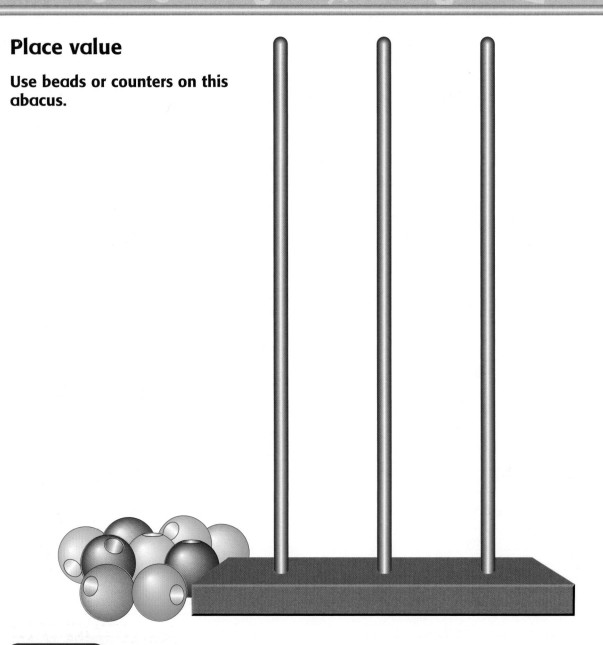

Starters

Use three beads.

1 Make the largest number.

2 Make the smallest number.

3 Make three different odd numbers.

4 Make three different even numbers.

5 Make two numbers between 200 and 300.

Practice

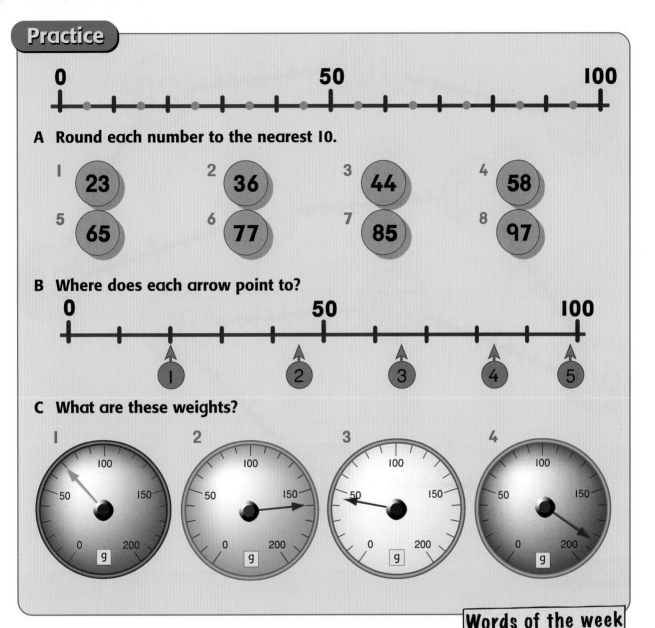

0   **50**   **100**

A Round each number to the nearest 10.

1 **23**   2 **36**   3 **44**   4 **58**

5 **65**   6 **77**   7 **85**   8 **97**

B Where does each arrow point to?

0   **50**   **100**

1   2   3   4   5

C What are these weights?

1   2   3   4

Challenge

Place three beads on the abacus.

How many different numbers can you make?

Write them in order.

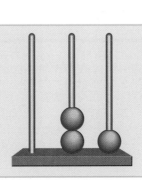

Words of the week

abacus

nearest

approximately

round off

37

Addition

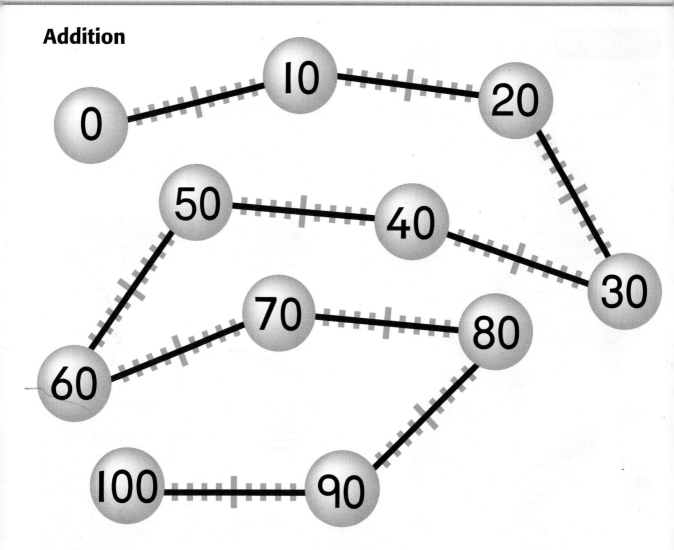

Use the number line to help you.

1		**2**		**3**	
68 + 7 = ☐		42 + ☐ = 58		☐ + 5 = 51	
45 + 8 = ☐		54 + ☐ = 67		☐ + 8 = 47	
36 + 9 = ☐		68 + ☐ = 74		☐ + 6 = 63	
77 + 7 = ☐		86 + ☐ = 95		☐ + 7 = 74	
56 + 6 = ☐		75 + ☐ = 86		☐ + 9 = 91	

Practice

A Total these.

1	3	4	8		2	5	7	9		3	8	4	9		4	3	6	7

1 | 3 | 4 | 8 | 2 | 5 | 7 | 9 | 3 | 8 | 4 | 9 | 4 | 3 | 6 | 7 |

5 | 8 | 5 | 8 | 6 | 9 | 6 | 2 | 7 | 4 | 3 | 7 | 5 | 8 | 2 | 8 | 9 | 7 |

9 | 1 | 5 | 8 | 9 | 10 | 2 | 6 | 8 | 5 | 11 | 6 | 6 | 6 | 6 | 12 | 3 | 8 | 7 | 7 |

B Total these. Look for the 10.

1 | 7 | 8 | 3 | 2 | 9 | 4 | 6 | 3 | 5 | 8 | 5 | 4 | 12 | 7 | 8 |

5 | 9 | 14 | 6 | 6 | 6 | 8 | 2 | 4 | 7 | 5 | 8 | 5 | 3 | 8 | 9 | 8 | 6 | 1 |

9 | 14 | 8 | 6 | 2 | 10 | 18 | 8 | 2 | 2 |

C Use the number line to help.

Check each answer.

1	46 + 30	2	54 + 20	3	71 + 20	4	19 + 50	5	25 + 70
6	56 + 23	7	42 + 35	8	12 + 65	9	74 + 15	10	28 + 61
11	47 + 13	12	36 + 24	13	55 + 25	14	61 + 19	15	38 + 52

D Use the number line to help.

Check each answer.

1	58 + 26	2	18 + 39	3	36 + 36	4	47 + 38	5	67 + 28
6	48 + 48	7	35 + 27	8	53 + 29	9	16 + 76	10	59 + 29
11	72 + 19	12	55 + 38	13	68 + 27	14	34 + 58	15	25 + 58

Words of the week
total, calculate,
tens, ones

Challenge

1 28 + ☐ = 94   2 16 + ☐ = 71   3 35 + ☐ = 82   4 49 + ☐ = 92

5 44 + ☐ = 71   6 46 + 67 = ☐   7 76 + 76 = ☐   8 38 + 85 = ☐

9 97 + 86 = ☐   10 62 + 59 = ☐

Addition and subtraction

Use two sets of digit cards.

Practice

A Put + or − to make these true.

1 16 ☐ 11 ☐ 2 = 7   2 18 ☐ 12 ☐ 6 = 12   3 6 ☐ 14 ☐ 12 = 8

4 7 ☐ 7 ☐ 6 = 20   5 15 ☐ 3 ☐ 4 = 8   6 16 ☐ 5 ☐ 9 = 12

7 12 ☐ 12 ☐ 8 = 16   8 18 ☐ 3 ☐ 10 = 25   9 9 ☐ 8 ☐ 7 = 24

B Make each number up to the next 100.

1 395 + ☐   2 415 + ☐   3 801 + ☐   4 638 + ☐

5 527 + ☐   6 177 + ☐   7 286 + ☐   8 555 + ☐

9 452 + ☐   10 938 + ☐   11 216 + ☐   12 404 + ☐

13 319 + ☐   14 826 + ☐   15 858 + ☐

C What are the answers?

1 393 + 4   2 216 + 3   3 501 + 7   4 642 + 5

5 872 + 7   6 387 − 2   7 496 − 4   8 725 − 5

9 899 − 7   10 648 − 6   11 642 + 8   12 574 + 6

13 315 + 5   14 648 + 2   15 537 + 3

D What are the answers?

1 400 + 36   2 700 + 54   3 200 + 96   4 500 + 17

5 600 + 92   6 300 − 2   7 400 − 6   8 900 − 5

9 800 − 3   10 200 − 4   11 400 + 300   12 600 + 200

13 500 + 500   16 700 + 200   15 200 + 700

Words of the week

sign
symbol
operation

Challenge

Put numbers in the spaces.

Each side must add up to the same amount.

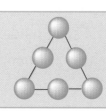

41

Money and problems

Starters

Find the cost of:

1 $\frac{1}{2}$ kg of apples.

2 $\frac{1}{2}$ kg of grapes.

3 Two oranges and a melon.

4 $\frac{1}{2}$ kg of grapes and 2 kg of potatoes.

5 $\frac{1}{2}$ kg of tomatoes and a pineapple.

Find the change from £5 after buying these:

6 Six oranges.

7 A pineapple and a melon.

8 1 kg of grapes.

9 1 kg of apples and $\frac{1}{2}$ kg of tomatoes.

10 2 lettuces and 1 kg of bananas.

Practice

A **A bag holds 48 onions.**

1 How many onions are left after 15 have been used?

2 How many people can have 2 onions each?

3 How many onions are in 2 bags?

4 How many bags are needed for 100 onions?

B 1 Tickets cost 75p each.
What will the cost be for two?
How much change from £2?

2 Jayne has a 50p coin and four
20p coins.
She buys an 80p ice cream.
How much has she left?

3 Philip bought five packets of sweets.
Each packet cost 70p each.
What was his change from £5?

4 Sweets cost 45p a packet.
How many packets can be bought
for £2?

5 Mandy and Li are sharing 90p.
Mandy must have 10p more than Li.
How much will each have?

6 Tom has 35p.
Ben has twice as much as Tom.
How much do they have
altogether?

C

Write in pence. | £1.20 | £4.75 | £3.06 | £7.10 | £9.36 | £8.86 |

Write in pounds. | 304p | 814p | 700p | 475p | 639p | 999p |

Challenge

You have £5.

Which three presents
could you buy?

£1.60

£1.90

£2.50

£1.40

£2.30

£1.70

**Words of
the week**

calculate
method
amount

43

Shape and space

Use cubes. Build these models.

Sort the models.

1 Make different models from
   four cubes.

   Sort the models into two sets.

2 Use three colours of cubes.

   Make a symmetrical pattern.

3 Make these two shapes:

   Put them together.

   Which shapes can you make?

Practice

A Draw these on squared paper.

Finish the shapes so that they are symmetrical.

Colour them to make a symmetrical pattern.

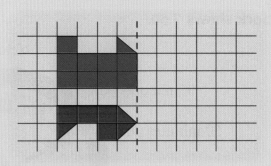

B Which shape do you land on?

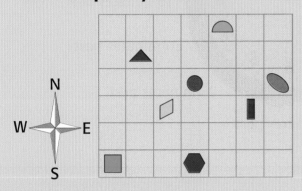

	Start	Move
1	square	3E ➡ 2N ➡ 1W
2	semicircle	5S ➡ 1W
3	oval	4W ➡ 3S ➡ 2W
4	rectangle	3N ➡ 1E ➡ 2S
5	hexagon	2N ➡ 2W ➡ 2N

C Look at the grid above.

Describe these journeys. You must not pass over another shape.

From	To
circle	semicircle
oval	square
square	rhombus
semicircle	hexagon
triangle	rectangle

Words to help

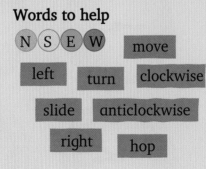

N S E W move left turn clockwise slide anticlockwise right hop

Words of the week

symmetrical
semicircle
compass
points

Challenge

Which letters of the alphabet have line symmetry?

Write the longest word you can using letters that have a line of symmetry.

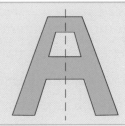

45

Time and weight

This clock shows 7.50.

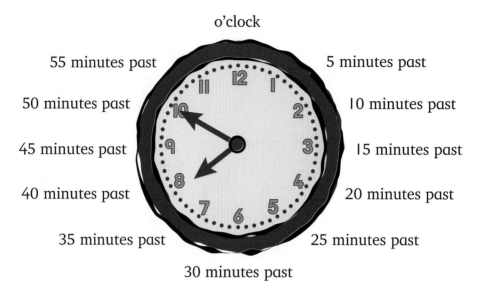

o'clock

55 minutes past   5 minutes past

50 minutes past   10 minutes past

45 minutes past   15 minutes past

40 minutes past   20 minutes past

35 minutes past   25 minutes past

30 minutes past

Starters

Which times do these clocks show?

A   B   C   D

E   F   G   H

All the times are in the afternoon or evening.

1 What is one hour later than D?   **2** What is one hour later than F?

3 Which clock says the latest time?   **4** Which clock says the earliest time?

5 How long is the time from F to B?

Practice

A Find out:

1 How many 500 g weights balance 1 kg.
2 How many 200 g weights balance 1 kg.
3 How many 100 g weights balance 1 kg.
4 How many 50 g weights balance 1 kg.

B What measurement is shown on the scales?

1  2  3  4

C 1 1 kg = ☐ g   2 1 kg and 200 g = ☐ g
   $\frac{1}{2}$ kg = ☐ g   2 kg and 500 g = ☐ g
   2 kg = ☐ g   3 kg and 250 g = ☐ g

3 400 g + 600 g = ☐ kg   600 g + 600 g = ☐ kg and ☐ g
500 g + 800 g = ☐ kg and ☐ g

Jess	24 kg
Conrad	26 kg
Sunita	20 kg
Louise	28 kg
Francis	25 kg

D 1 Who is the heaviest?
2 Who is the lightest?
3 How much heavier is Louise than Francis?
4 How much heavier is Conrad than Jess?

Challenge

Make the same-size bags from different papers.

Test the strengths by adding weights.
Make sure the tests are fair.

Words of the week
kilogram
gram
relationship

Review

A

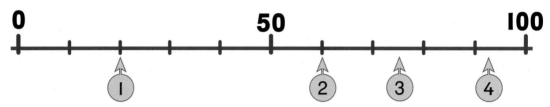

0   **50**   **100**

Round each number to the nearest 10.

79   44   55   81   96

B Where does each arrow point to?

0   **50**   **100**

1   2   3   4

C Total these numbers.

1

7   9   6

2

5   8   6   4

D Answer these sums.

1   35 + 20   2   27 + 32   3   54 + 16

E Answer these sums.

1   26 + 35   2   46 + 46   3   64 + 29

F Make each number up to the next 100.

1   426 + ☐   2   488 + ☐   3   719 + ☐

G **1** One book costs £2.50.
What will three books cost?

2 Two books cost £5.
What will one book cost?

H **Name each shape.**

1  **2** 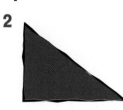 **3** 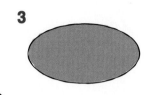 **4**  **5**

I **Name each shape.**

1 **2** **3** **4**  **5**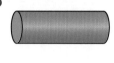

J **What do the clocks say?**

1  **2**  **3**  **4**

K **Measure each line to the nearest cm.**

1 ━━━━━━━━━

2 ━━━━━━━━━━━━━━━━━━

3 ━━━━━━━━━━━━━━━

49

Numbers and counting patterns

176	289	342	999	500
457	250	450	618	550
400	110	803	199	852
645	375	210	700	305

Starters

Look at the numbers on the grid.

1 Write the largest odd number.

2 Write the smallest even number.

3 Write the multiples of 5.

4 Write the multiples of 10.

5 Write the multiples of 100.

6 Write the largest multiple of 2.

7 Write the numbers that are less than 300.

8 Write the numbers that are more than 700.

9 Write the numbers that are between 400 and 500.

10 Write the numbers that are one less than a multiple of 100.

Practice

A Copy and complete these sequences.

I	45	55	65	☐	☐	☐	☐	2	37	47	57	☐	☐	☐ ☐
3	74	84	94	☐	☐	☐	☐	4	68	78	88	☐	☐	☐ ☐
5	71	81	91	☐	☐	☐	☐	6	125	135	145	☐	☐	☐ ☐
7	206	216	226	☐	☐	☐	☐	8	378	388	398	☐	☐	☐ ☐
9	763	773	783	☐	☐	☐	☐	10	870	880	890	☐	☐	☐ ☐

B I Count on 4 from each number.

46   125   208   199   296

2 Count on 3 from each number.

84   176   307   298   394

3 Count on 5 from each number.

77   145   209   457   595

Challenge

Look at two multiples of 10, such as 80 and 90.

I Are there always more odd than even numbers between them?

2 What if the two multiples of 10 are not consecutive?

3 Write about what you find out.

Words of the week

sequences
number
pattern
multiples

Addition and problems

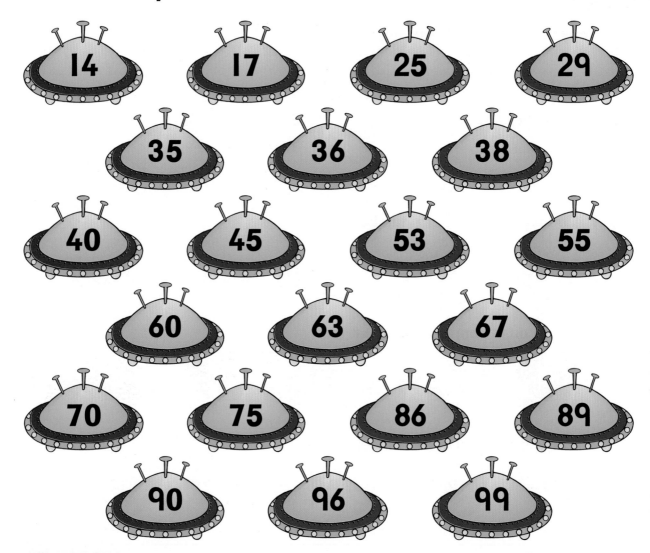

14   17   25   29

35   36   38

40   45   53   55

60   63   67

70   75   86   89

90   96   99

Starters

1   Find pairs of numbers that total 100.

2   Find pairs of numbers that total more than 100.

3   Find pairs of numbers that total less than 50.

4   Total the largest and smallest numbers.

5   Total the numbers between 20 and 30.

6   Total the numbers between 30 and 40.

Practice

A Break up each number into tens and ones: 37 = 30 + 7

| 46 | 29 | 56 | 37 | 48 | 68 | 75 | 84 |

B Answer these sums.

1 36 + 48	**2** 58 + 27	**3** 18 + 57	**4** 47 + 29
5 62 + 28	**6** 52 + 39	**7** 66 + 17	**8** 45 + 35
9 72 + 17	**10** 29 + 29		

C Answer these sums.

1 68 + 54	**2** 35 + 75	**3** 94 + 26	**4** 54 + 78
5 93 + 68	**6** 75 + 85	**7** 46 + 93	**8** 72 + 89
9 64 + 64	**10** 38 + 83		

D Total each set of numbers.

1 12 – 14 – 19   **2** 17 – 18 – 16   **3** 24 – 16 – 15   **4** 24 – 22 – 23

5 17 – 23 – 34   **6** 15 – 26 – 28   **7** 14 – 25 – 31   **8** 26 – 34 – 46

E **1** Three shirts cost £17, £14 and £18. What is the total cost?

2 Two comics cost 49p and 99p. What is the total cost?

3 How much change will I get from £5 if I spend £1.60 and £1.90?

4 Books cost £4.50 each. What will three books cost?

5 £7.50 is shared equally between two people. How much will each get?

6 How many 19p stamps can be bought for £1?

Challenge

Use three of these numbers at a time.

Find all the different totals you can.

18   53   64   104   98

Words of the week

hundreds boundary

tens boundary

Division

Start from 0.

1 How many hops of 2 to reach

12 16 20 24

2 How many hops of 3 to reach

9 12 18 30

3 How many hops of 4 to reach

12 20 28 36

4 How many hops of 5 to reach

15 30 35 45

Practice

A Answer these.

1 $10 \div 2$	2 $12 \div 4$	3 $16 \div 4$	4 $25 \div 5$
5 $18 \div 3$	6 $24 \div 3$	7 $18 \div 2$	8 $35 \div 5$
9 $40 \div 4$	10 $27 \div 3$	11 $40 \div 5$	12 $16 \div 2$

B

1 $\square \div 2 = 4$ 2 $\square \div 5 = 4$ 3 $\square \div 3 = 4$ 4 $\square \div 4 = 4$

5 $\square \div 3 = 8$ 6 $\square \div 4 = 8$ 7 $\square \div 5 = 9$ 8 $\square \div 4 = 6$

9 $\square \div 3 = 7$ 10 $\square \div 4 = 5$

C

1 $12 \div \square = 6$ 2 $15 \div \square = 5$ 3 $24 \div \square = 6$ 4 $35 \div \square = 7$

5 $50 \div \square = 10$ 6 $9 \div \square = 3$ 7 $36 \div \square = 9$ 8 $27 \div \square = 9$

9 $18 \div \square = 9$ 10 $40 \div \square = 10$

D

1 Share £12 between 2.   2 Divide £24 by 4.   3 Share £20 into 5s.

4 Divide £36 into 4.   5 How many 2s in 24?   6 How many 3s in 33?

7 How many 4s in 48?   8 How many 5s in 65?   9 Is 16 a multiple of 2?

10 Is 16 a multiple of 3?   11 Is 16 a multiple of 4?   12 Is 16 a multiple of 5?

E

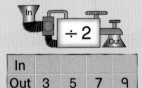

In				
Out	3	5	7	9

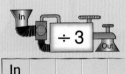

In				
Out	2	6	9	10

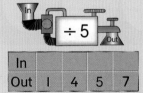

In				
Out	1	4	5	7

Challenge

$\square \div 2 = \triangle$ $\square \div 3 = \triangle$ $\square \div 4 = \triangle$

The numbers in the $\square$ are more than 30.

What could the numbers be?

Find three answers for each division sum.

Words of the week

divide

share

remainder

Fractions

Use counters.

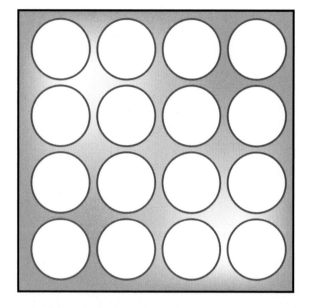 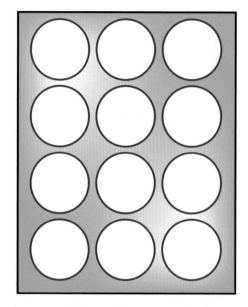

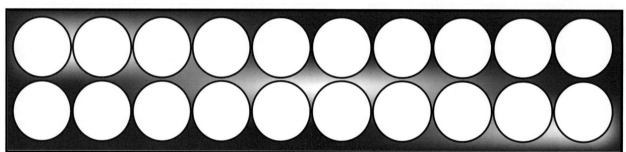

Starters

1

$1 \text{ whole} = \dfrac{\square}{\square} + \dfrac{\square}{\square}$ What could the two fractions be?

2

$\text{A half} = \dfrac{\square}{\square}$ What could the fraction be?

Practice

A About how much of each cake has been eaten?

1   2   3   4  5

B

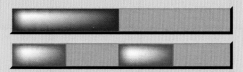

1 How many $\frac{1}{2}$s make a whole?   2 How many $\frac{1}{4}$s make a whole?

3 How many $\frac{1}{10}$s make a whole?   4 How many $\frac{1}{4}$s make a half?

5 How many $\frac{1}{10}$s make a half?

C Estimate how many marbles are in the jar.

1 This jar holds 100.      2 This jar holds 50.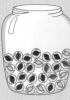

3 This jar holds 16.      4 This jar holds 60.

Challenge

Make some squares and rectangles with cubes.

$\frac{1}{4}$ must be red and $\frac{3}{4}$ must be white.

Show what you find out.

Words of the week

whole

fraction

equal

parts

Bar charts

Use counters.

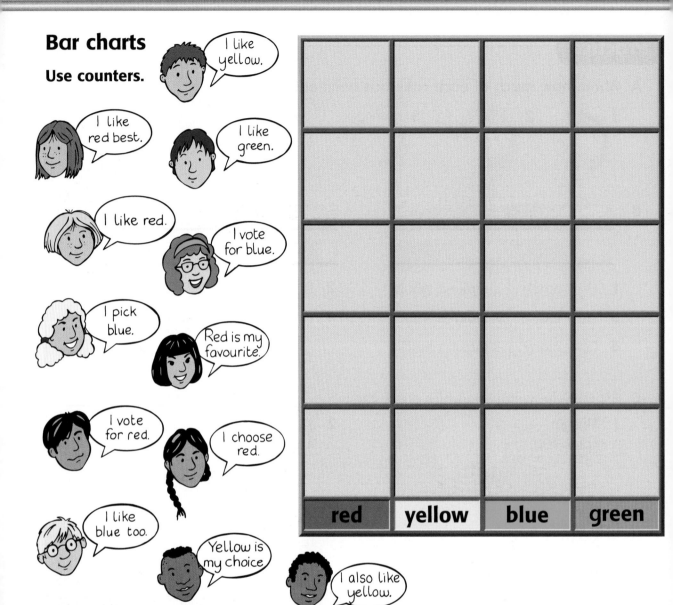

1 What is the most popular colour?
2 What is the least popular colour?
3 How many children like yellow best?
4 How many children like blue best?
5 What is the difference between the most and the least favourite colours?
6 How many children were asked about their favourite colours?

Practice

A Birds seen at our bird table

	0	1	2	3	4	5	6	7	8	9
blue tit										
robin										
sparrow										
dove										
blackbird										
starling										

1 How many sparrows visited?

2 Which was the most frequent visitor?

3 Which bird was seen least?

4 How many blue tits were seen?

5 How many more sparrows were there than doves?

6 How many birds were seen altogether?

B Our favourite drinks

	0	2	4	6	8	10	12	14	16
squash									
milk									
water									
cola									
tea									
coffee									
none									

1 What was the favourite drink?

2 How many liked squash best?

3 How many liked tea best?

4 How many liked water best?

5 How many did not have a favourite drink?

6 How many people were asked?

Words of the week

bar

chart

axis

Challenge

Ask about favourite types of drink.

Show the information in a table.

Review

A Round each number to the nearest 10.

1 **36**   2 **72**   3 **65**   4 **87**   5 **93**

40

B Total these numbers.

1 **37 – 8**   2 **50 – 70**   3 **32 – 54**   4 **28 – 37**

C How much change from £10?

1  £2   £3.50

2  £4   £3.40

3  £1.50   £1.50

4  £4.50   £3.50

D Which of these are right angles?

1   2   3   4   5

 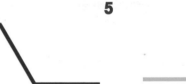

E

1   $55 + \boxed{} = 100$

2   $32 + \boxed{} = 100$

3   $78 + \boxed{} = 100$

4   $21 + \boxed{} = 100$

F Measure these lines to the nearest $\frac{1}{2}$ cm.

1 ━━━━━━━━━ 2 ━━━

3 ━━━━━━━━━

G Answer these.

1 $7 \times 10 = \boxed{}$ 2 $3 \times 4 = \boxed{}$ 3 $5 \times 5 = \boxed{}$ 4 $2 \times 9 = \boxed{}$

5 $\boxed{} \times 3 = 9$ 6 $\boxed{} \times 5 = 35$ 7 $2 \times \boxed{} = 20$ 8 $5 \times \boxed{} = 45$

H Answer these.

1 $12 \div 2 = \boxed{}$ 2 $25 \div 5 = \boxed{}$ 3 $80 \div 10 = \boxed{}$ 4 $6 \div 3 = \boxed{}$

5 $\boxed{} \div 5 = 4$ 6 $\boxed{} \div 2 = 8$ 7 $12 \div \boxed{} = 6$ 8 $90 \div \boxed{} = 9$

I Estimate the fraction that is coloured.

1  2 3 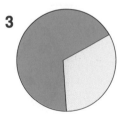 4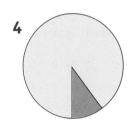

J What do these say?

1  2 3

Do you remember?

1 **What is the next number in this sequence?**

> **5**   **8**   **11**   **14**   ☐

(a) 15   (b) 16   (c) 17   (d) 18

2 **What is the missing number?**

$$100 = \boxed{} + 55$$

(a) 35   (b) 45   (c) 55   (d) 65

3 **What is the next odd number after** **239** **?**

(a) 240   (b) 241   (c) 242   (d) 243

4 **What does this time say?**

(a) 6.55   (b) 7.55   (c) 8.55   (d) 8.50

5 **What is 9 less than** **86** **?**

(a) 75   (b) 76   (c) 77   (d) 78

6 Name this shape.

   a cuboid   **b** prism   **c** triangle   **d** pyramid

---

7 Estimate the size of this angle.

   a right angle

   b more than a right angle

   c less than a right angle

---

8 This shape has been cut into quarters.

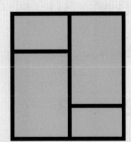

   a True   **b** Not true

---

9 The change from £5 will be

   a £1.20   **b** £2.20   **c** £3.20

---

10 The length of this line is

   a 6 cm   **b** $6\frac{1}{2}$ cm   **c** 7 cm

Check your answers on page 96. ✓

Place value

Use counters.

1000	2000	3000	4000	5000	6000	7000	8000	9000
100	200	300	400	500	600	700	800	900
10	20	30	40	50	60	70	80	90
1	2	3	4	5	6	7	8	9

Starters

$$425 = 400 + 20 + 5$$

1 What will you cover to make

356   407   680   564   733

2 Which numbers are these?

200 + 50 + 3   300 + 60 + 7

600 + 70   400 + 2

800 + 90 + 7

3 What is missing?

$532 = \boxed{} + 30 + 2$ $471 = 400 + \boxed{} + 1$ $752 = 700 + 50 + \boxed{}$

$668 = 600 + \boxed{} + 8$ $719 = \boxed{} + 10 + \boxed{}$

Practice

```
0                    500                    1000
├──┼──┼──┼──┼──┼──┼──┼──┼──┼──┤
```

A Round each number to the nearest 100.

1 **260**   2 **410**   3 **870**   4 **650**

5 **240**   6 **590**   7 **770**   8 **950**

B Round each number to the nearest 100.

1 **155**   2 **275**   3 **425**   4 **499**

5 **619**   6 **772**   7 **348**   8 **791**

C Round to the nearest £.

1 **£4.60**   2 **£3.75**   3 **£6.25**   4 **£7.50**

5 **£1.99**   6 **£3.19**   7 **£7.04**   8 **£5.48**

D Which numbers do you think the arrows point to?

```
0                    500                    1000
├──┼──┼──┼──┼──┼──┼──┼──┼──┼──┤
    ①      ②           ③      ④         ⑤
```

Words of the week
nearest
closer to
approximately

Challenge

2 **4** **8**   **3** **1** **7**

Write three different numbers.
Only use even digits.

Write three different numbers.
Only use odd digits.

Put your six numbers in order.

Adding and subtracting

Cover pairs of numbers.

Add them.

19	49	61	29	71
81	59	89	21	79
31	91	69	99	51

47	34	55	73	26
58	92	38	74	77
25	65	62	44	85

Starters

Answer these sums.

1 39 + 26	2 26 + 19	3 45 + 31	4 39 + 36	5 59 + 18
6 68 + 19	7 38 + 51	8 64 + 79	9 26 + 61	10 39 + 76
11 19 + 29	12 49 + 59	13 29 + 89	14 69 + 79	15 99 + 89

Practice

A Total each set.

1 (8) (9) (4) 2 (12) (5) (8) 3 (7) (8) (13) 4 (5) (8) (7)

5 (9) (9) (9) 6 (15) (5) (8) 7 (14) (8) (6) 8 (8) (13) (7)

B Each total must be 1000.

1 ☐ + 200   2 ☐ + 900   3 ☐ + 500   4 ☐ + 400   5 ☐ + 100

6 300 + ☐   7 600 + ☐   8 800 + ☐   9 700 + ☐   10 400 + ☐

C

1 14 + ☐ = 19   2 98 − ☐ = 93   3 ☐ + 8 = 12

   14 + ☐ = 29   98 − ☐ = 83   ☐ + 80 = 120

   14 + ☐ = 39   98 − ☐ = 73   ☐ + 800 = 1200

   14 + ☐ = 49   98 − ☐ = 63   40 + ☐ = 120

   14 + ☐ = 59   98 − ☐ = 53   4 + ☐ = 12

D Find the missing numbers.

1 200 + 900 = ☐   2 600 − 4 = ☐   3 300 + 27 = ☐

   600 + 800 = ☐   400 − 7 = ☐   400 + 36 = ☐

   700 + 700 = ☐   300 − 9 = ☐   700 + 45 = ☐

   500 + 600 = ☐   800 − 5 = ☐   800 + 97 = ☐

Challenge

Explore three hops to reach 500

$$180 + \boxed{} + \triangle = 500$$

Words of the week

answer

thousand

relationship

Problems

PARTY TIME

£1·80

COLA

3 Pack CRISPS 99p

£1·15

Cherry Buns £1·25

£1·20 YOGHURT

Biscuits £1·99

Starters

There are 30 children at the party.

1 How many boxes of biscuits are needed for each child to have a biscuit?

2 How many packs of buns are needed?

3 How many packs of cola are needed?

4 How many large packets of crisps are needed?

5 Swiss rolls are cut into 8 slices. How many swiss rolls are needed?

6 What does one can of cola cost?

7 What does one packet of crisps cost?

8 What does one pot of yoghurt cost?

9 How much will the cola cost for the party?

10 How much will the swiss rolls cost for the party?

Practice

A What is the change from £10 for each bill?

1
apples	£1.30
potatoes	£1.65
peas	£1.15

2
papers	£2.30
magazine	£1.20
book	£5.00

3
cap	£1.99
shirt	£2.99
shorts	£3.99

B Choose a problem.

Make up a number story about money.

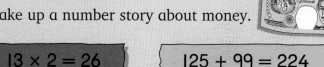

$13 \times 2 = 26$ $125 + 99 = 224$ $200 - 145 = 55$

C Write a sum for each of these.

1 James buys 3 books.
They cost 40p each.
What change will he get from £5?

2 Adult tickets are £3 each.
Children's tickets are half price.
What will 2 adults and 1 child cost?

3 Pencil sharpeners cost 49p.
How many can I buy for £2?
What will my change be?

4 Six eggs cost £1.20.
What will 12 eggs cost?

5 Potatoes cost 24p for a kilogram.
What will $\frac{1}{2}$ kg cost?

6 Zoom bars cost 30p each and
Swish bars cost 40p each.
What will two bars of each cost?

D How much more to make £1?

1 (45p)   2 (58p)   3 (63p)   4 (19p)   5 (26p)   6 (77p)

Challenge

2p   5p   10p

Investigate stickers you can buy for 20p.

Words of the week
investigate
check
solve
method

69

Adding

Talk about these jumps.

How big are the jumps?

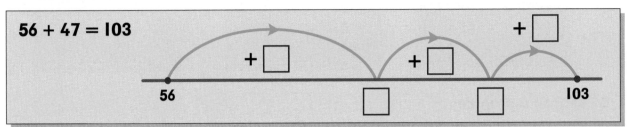

$56 + 47 = 103$

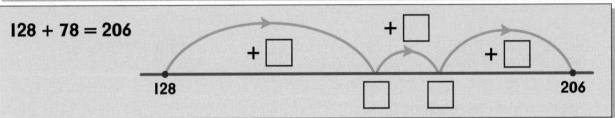

$128 + 78 = 206$

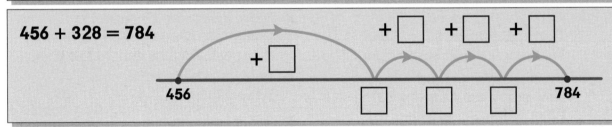

$456 + 328 = 784$

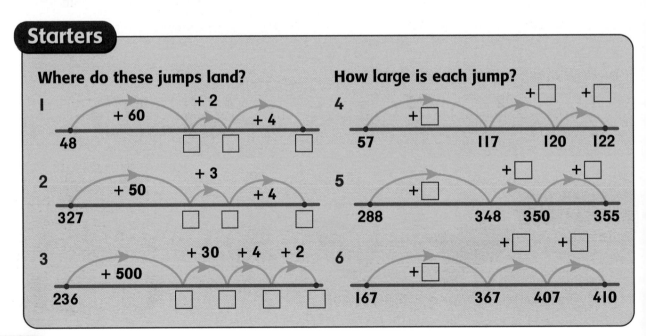

Starters

Where do these jumps land?

1

+ 60   + 2   + 4

48

2

+ 50   + 3   + 4

327

3

+ 500   + 30   + 4   + 2

236

How large is each jump?

4

+☐   +☐   +☐

57   117   120   122

5

+☐   +☐   +☐

288   348   350   355

6

+☐   +☐   +☐

167   367   407   410

Practice

A
1 56 + 87   2 38 + 75   3 28 + 67   4 56 + 56   5 28 + 95
6 28 + 74   7 66 + 38   8 54 + 79   9 68 + 68   10 43 + 58

B
1 236 + 58   2 178 + 65   3 209 + 86   4 423 + 78   5 536 + 59
6 278 + 57   7 135 + 88   8 658 + 38   9 455 + 98   10 826 + 36

C
1 423 + 154   2 438 + 165   3 174 + 245   4 368 + 422
5 366 + 244   6 565 + 385   7 266 + 392   8 156 + 528

D
1   67   2   38   3   54   4   76   5   97
   + 24   + 57   + 69   + 46   + 38
   ____   ____   ____   ____   ____

6   36   7   77   8   54   9   34   10   46
   + 94   + 66   + 67   + 86   + 35
   ____   ____   ____   ____   ____

E
1   143   2   543   3   647   4   345   5   726
   + 62   + 72   + 28   + 39   + 56
   ____   ____   ____   ____   ____

6   238   7   578   8   446   9   375   10   734
   + 96   + 68   + 87   + 88   + 77
   ____   ____   ____   ____   ____

Challenge

Write two numbers more than 100.

Show how to make two hops between them.

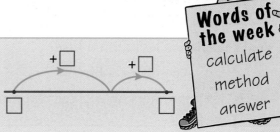

Words of the week
calculate
method
answer

71

Capacity

1 litre = 1000 millilitres

1 l = 1000 ml

$\frac{1}{2}$ l = 500 ml

Starters

1 Which holds most?

2 Which holds least?

3 Which holds more than a litre?

4 Which holds less than a litre?

5 Which holds about a litre?

6 Which containers hold about the same?

Practice

A How much is in each jug?

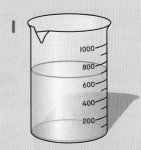  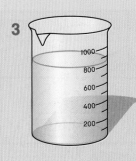 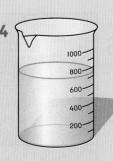

B Look at the jugs above.

1 How much more is in the last jug than the second?

2 How much more is in the third jug than the first?

3 How much must be added to the second jug to make 1 litre?

4 How much must be added to the fourth jug to make 1 litre?

5 Which jug is nearest to $\frac{1}{2}$ litre?

C 1 A teapot holds 750 ml.
A teacup holds 200 ml.
How many cups of tea from a full pot?

2 A medicine bottle holds 150 ml.
A medicine spoon holds 5 ml.
Jo has two spoons of medicine each day.
How long will the medicine last?

Words of the week

capacity
litre
millilitre
half litre

Challenge

Put an elastic band on a bottle to show where you think 200 ml is.

Check and see.

Try with different bottles.

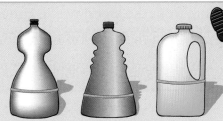

Shape and space

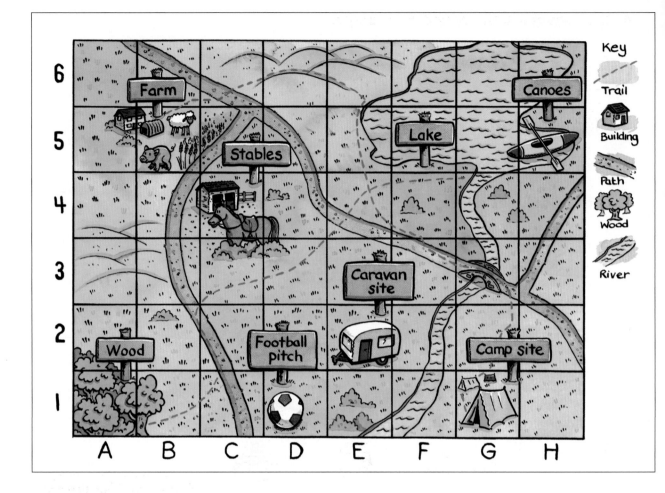

1 What will you find at E2, H5 and B5?

2 Write the positions of the football pitch, the camp site and the stables.

3 Describe a route from the wood to the canoes.

4 Describe a route from the caravan to the farm.

5 Describe a route from C1 to the bridge keeping to the paths.

Practice

A Talk about symmetry and right angles.

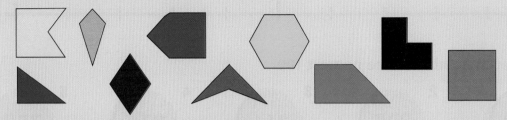

B Record the angles in a table like this one.

right angle	
more than a right angle	
less than a right angle	

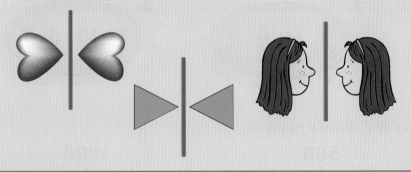

C Draw a mirror line.

Sketch a shape and its reflection.

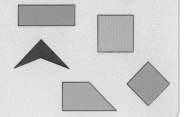

Words of the week

symmetry
right angle
reflection
quadrilaterals

Challenge

Make a set of quadrilaterals.

Sort them in a table like this one.

symmetrical	non-symmetrical

75

Review

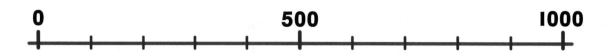

0   500   1000

A Round each number to the nearest 100.

1   450   2   275   3   344   4   874   5   738

B Write these numbers in order.

237   732   327   723   273   372

C Total each set.

1   9   7   12

2   7   11   9   2

3   5   13   5   7

D Estimate which numbers the arrows point to.

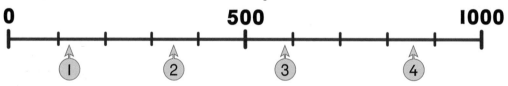

0   500   1000

E Answer the sums.

1   $\square$ + 200 = 1000   **2**   200 + 800 = $\square$ **3**   700 + 800 = $\square$

F **1** 56 + 37   **2** 46 + 46   **3** 72 + 58   **4** 63 + 88

G **1**   127   **2**   368   **3**   629   **4**   718
          +   58   +   75   +   65   +   96
        ——————   ——————   ——————   ——————

          ——————   ——————   ——————   ——————

H What is the time?

1

2

3

I Name these shapes.

1

2
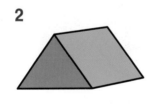

3

4

5
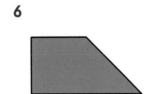

6
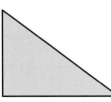

7
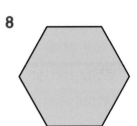

8

Numbers

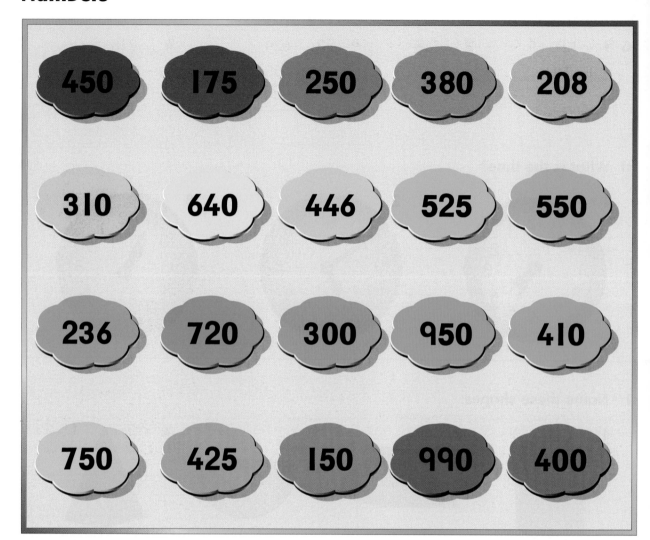

450	175	250	380	208
310	640	446	525	550
236	720	300	950	410
750	425	150	990	400

Starters

Use the grid.

1 Write the largest odd number.
2 Write the largest even number.
3 Write pairs that total 1000.
4 Write numbers between 500 and 700.
5 Write numbers less than 300.
6 Write multiples of 2.
7 Write multiples of 5.
8 Write multiples of 10.
9 Write multiples of 50.
10 Write multiples of 100.

Practice

A Copy and complete these sequences.

1   68   70   72   74   □ □ □

2   95   90   85   80   □ □ □

3   145   150   155   160   □ □ □

4   34   37   40   43   □ □ □

5   90   87   84   81   □ □ □

B Draw the tables.

Write the numbers.

1
multiple of 5	
not a multiple of 5	

75   135   556   205   54   352   60   765

2
multiple of 2	
not a multiple of 2	

64   310   652   999   45   253   86   198

C Are these TRUE?

1   Every odd number is always one more than an even number.

2   Adding two odd numbers always makes an even number.

3   A multiple of 2 is sometimes odd.

4   A multiple of 10 is always a multiple of 5 as well.

Challenge

  ③ ④ ⑤ are next door numbers.

Work out these next door numbers.

○ + ○ + ○ = 9   ○ + ○ + ○ + ○ = 18

○ + ○ + ○ = 21   ○ + ○ + ○ + ○ = 26

> **Words of the week**
> largest
> smallest
> multiples
> sequences

Remainders

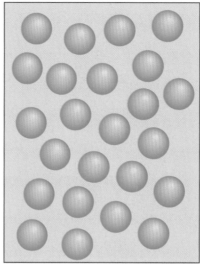

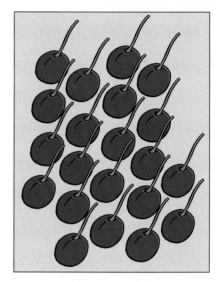

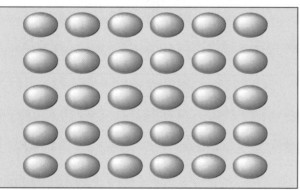

Which sets will have a remainder?

What will the remainder be each time?

1

I will gulp 2 at a time

2 I will gulp 3 at a time

3

I will gulp 4 at a time

4 I will gulp 5 at a time

Practice

A Answer these.

I 16 ÷ 3	2 15 ÷ 2	3 14 ÷ 4	4 21 ÷ 5	5 19 ÷ 4
6 37 ÷ 10	7 28 ÷ 5	8 76 ÷ 10	9 19 ÷ 3	10 26 ÷ 3
II 37 ÷ 4	12 84 ÷ 10	13 42 ÷ 5	14 25 ÷ 4	15 99 ÷ 10

B How much is left?

1 Share 24 between 5.   2 Cut 10 cm lengths from a 75 cm roll.

3 Divide 36 by 10.   4 Buy £2 tickets with £17.

5 Share 19 into threes.   6 Pour 5 ml spoons from a 35 ml bottle.

7 Divide 26 into fours.   8 Pack 72 eggs in boxes that hold 10.

9 Share 31 amongst 5.   10 Divide £2.30 into piles of 50p.

C 1 I have £37.   2 I have £32.
Tickets cost £5.   Books cost £4 each.
How many can I buy?   How many can I buy?

3 A cake box holds 10 cakes.   4 I have 17 sweets to share.
I have 37 cakes.   There are 3 children.
How many boxes can I fill?   How many will each receive?

D 1 A box holds 5 cakes.   2 A table sits 10 people
I have 47 cakes.   There are 45 children.
How many boxes will I need?   How many tables are needed?

Words of the week
divide
share
remainder

Challenge

What are the missing numbers?

$56 = 10 \times 5 + \boxed{}$ $87 = 10 \times \boxed{} + \boxed{}$ $19 = 5 \times 3 + \boxed{}$

$48 = 9 \times \boxed{} + \boxed{}$ $25 = 6 \times 4 + \boxed{}$ $93 = 10 \times \boxed{} + \boxed{}$

Money and problems

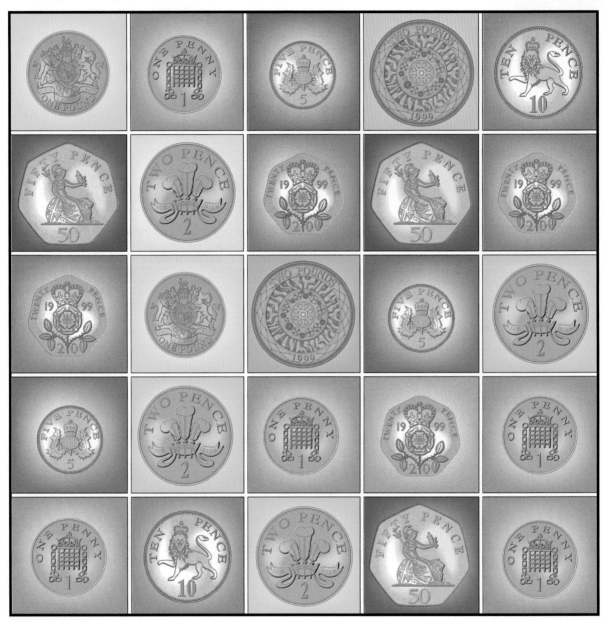

Which three coins give these totals? **Which four coins give these totals?**

1 £2.05	**2** £3.10	**3** £1.02	**6** £5.00	**7** £3.50	**8** £1.00
4 £0.60	**5** £1.70		**9** £1.06	**10** £2.80	

Practice

A **What are the missing numbers?**

1 $7 \times 100 = \boxed{}$	**2** $700 \div 100 = \boxed{}$	**3** $100 \div 10 = \boxed{}$	**4** $600 \div \boxed{} = 60$
$3 \times 100 = \boxed{}$	$900 \div 100 = \boxed{}$	$500 \div 10 = \boxed{}$	$500 \div \boxed{} = 5$
$5 \times 100 = \boxed{}$	$200 \div 100 = \boxed{}$	$600 \div 10 = \boxed{}$	$800 \div \boxed{} = 8$
$8 \times 100 = \boxed{}$	$400 \div 100 = \boxed{}$	$800 \div 10 = \boxed{}$	$400 \div \boxed{} = 40$
$6 \times 100 = \boxed{}$	$300 \div 100 = \boxed{}$	$700 \div 10 = \boxed{}$	$700 \div \boxed{} = 70$

B **Copy and complete the tables.**

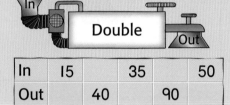

In	15		35		50
Out		40		90	

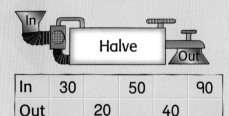

In	30		50		90
Out		20		40	

C

1 $60 \times 2 = \boxed{}$	**2** $20 \times \boxed{} = 100$	**3** $\boxed{} \times 10 = 700$
4 $30 = 3 \times \boxed{}$	**5** $32 \times 3 = \boxed{}$	**6** $14 \times \boxed{} = 28$
7 $\boxed{} \times 5 = 55$	**8** $26 = 13 \times \boxed{}$	

D **Choose a problem.**

Make up a number story about money.

$$400 \div \boxed{} = 4 \qquad 23 \times 3 = \boxed{} \qquad 13 \times \boxed{} = 39$$

Challenge

What are the missing signs?

$320 \boxed{} 10 = 32$	$400 \boxed{} 40 = 360$	$50 \boxed{} 30 = 1500$
$200 \boxed{} 600 = 800$	$240 \boxed{} 20 = 12$	$700 \boxed{} 2 = 350$

Words of the week

value
amount
notes
coins

Fractions

Estimate the fractions.

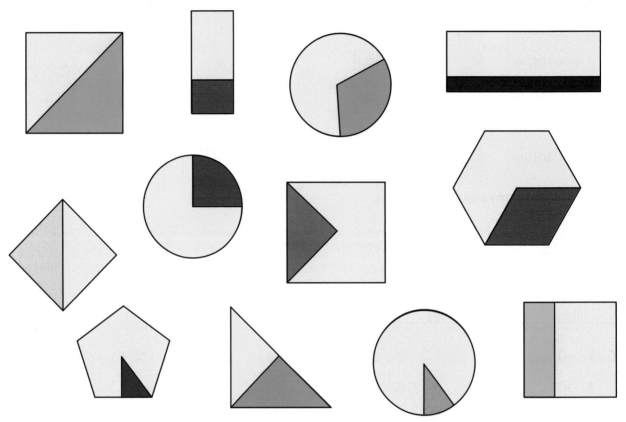

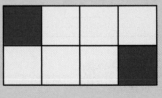
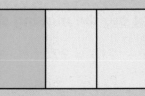

Starters

Write the fraction that is coloured.

1

2

3

4

5

6

Practice

A

0   1   2   3   4

1   Which fraction is half way between 1 and 2?

2   Which fraction is half way between 3 and 4?

3   Which fraction is half way between $\frac{1}{2}$ and 1?

4   Which fraction is half way between 2 and $2\frac{1}{2}$?

5   Which fraction is half way between 1 and 3?

6   Which fraction is half way between $1\frac{1}{2}$ and $2\frac{1}{2}$?

B

0   50   100

1   Find 60 on the line. Where is $\frac{1}{2}$ of 60?

2   Find 70 on the line. Where is $\frac{1}{2}$ of 70?

3   Find 30 on the line. Where is $\frac{1}{2}$ of 30?

4   Find 80 on the line. Where is $\frac{1}{2}$ of 80?

5   Estimate where 24 is. Estimate half way.

6   Estimate where 68 is. Estimate half way.

C   1 $1 = \dfrac{\boxed{}}{2}$ 2 $1 = \dfrac{\boxed{}}{3}$ 3 $1 = \dfrac{\boxed{}}{4}$ 4 $1 = \dfrac{\boxed{}}{10}$

    5   $\dfrac{1}{2} = \dfrac{\boxed{}}{4}$ 6 $\dfrac{1}{2} = \dfrac{\boxed{}}{10}$ 7 $\dfrac{1}{4} + \dfrac{1}{4} = \boxed{}$ 8 $\dfrac{1}{2} + \dfrac{1}{4} = \boxed{}$

Challenge

Draw round some shapes.

Colour in about $\frac{3}{4}$ of each shape.

Which shapes are easy?

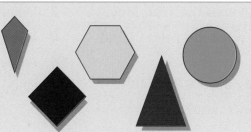

Words of the week

fraction

estimate

half way

Time and subtracting

MAY

Mon	Tue	Wed	Thu	Fri	Sat	Sun
		1	2	3	4	5
6	7	8	9	10	11	12
13	14	15	16	17	18	19
20	21	22	23	24	25	26
27	28	29	30	31		

Starters

1 On which day was the 15th May?

2 When was the third Tuesday in May?

3 What is one week later than 22nd May?

4 When was the first weekend in May?

5 On which day did 1st June fall?

6 On which day did 30th April fall?

7 What is today's date?

8 What is the date of your birthday?

Practice

A What are the missing numbers?

1 110 − 30 = ☐   **2** 120 − ☐ = 80   **3** ☐ − 40 = 90

130 − 90 = ☐   160 − ☐ = 50   ☐ − 80 = 70

126 − 40 = ☐   137 − ☐ = 87   ☐ − 70 = 68

131 − 70 = ☐   166 − ☐ = 56   ☐ − 50 = 74

B 84 − 56

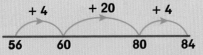

1 52 − 37   **2** 66 − 48   **3** 81 − 26   **4** 54 − 17   **5** 92 − 43

6 86 − 39   **7** 72 − 36   **8** 53 − 17   **9** 65 − 36   **10** 78 − 39

C 1 64   **2** 81   **3** 61   **4** 74   **5** 83
     − 36   − 37   − 46   − 25   − 57
    ____   ____   ____   ____   ____

6 85   **7** 63   **8** 57   **9** 92   **10** 56
     − 39   − 18   − 38   − 26   − 28
    ____   ____   ____   ____   ____

D 1 124   **2** 268   **3** 473   **4** 590   **5** 673
     − 18   − 39   − 86   − 75   − 58
    ____   ____   ____   ____   ____

6 236   **7** 417   **8** 805   **9** 628   **10** 738
     − 52   − 62   − 71   − 84   − 74
    ____   ____   ____   ____   ____

Challenge

 −   **Use these digits.**

Make different answers.

Words of the week

calendar
date

Diagrams

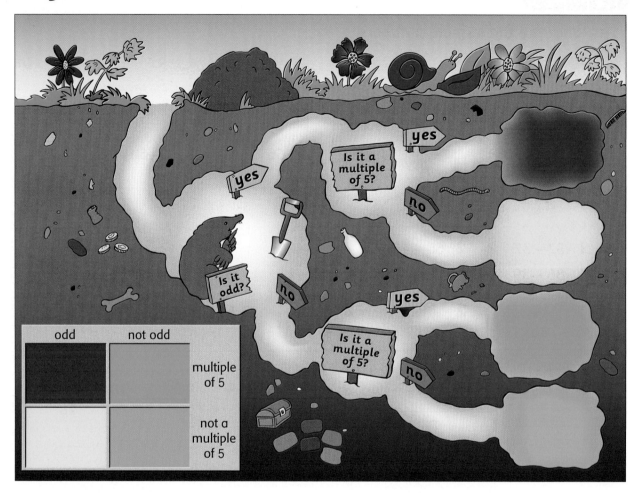

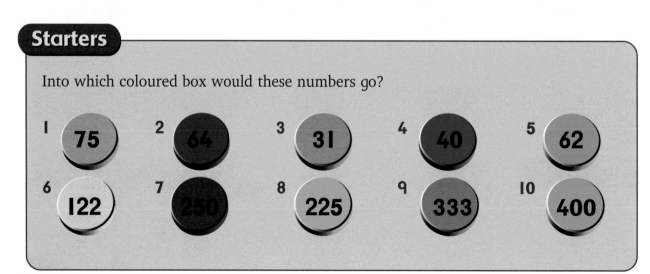

Starters

Into which coloured box would these numbers go?

1 **75** 2 **64** 3 **31** 4 **40** 5 **62**

6 **122** 7 **250** 8 **225** 9 **333** 10 **400**

Practice

A

quadrilaterals

Which part of the diagram: blue or yellow?

1 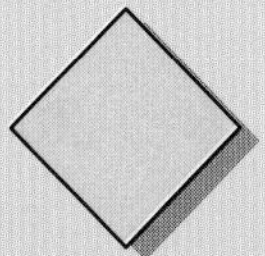   2 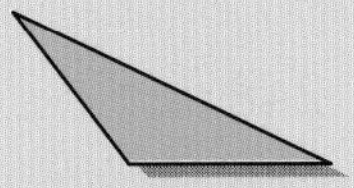   3    4 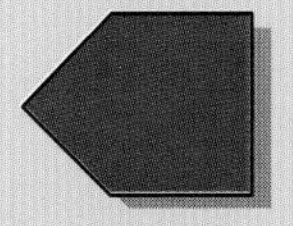   5

6    7 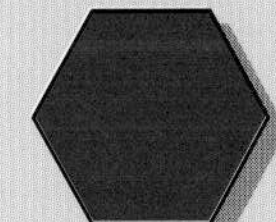   8 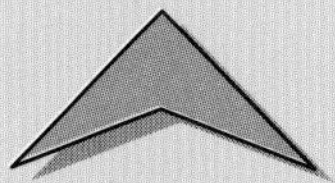   9 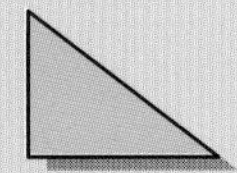   10

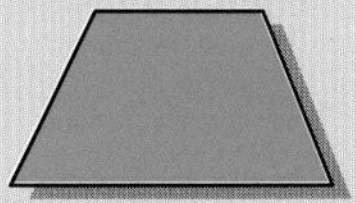

B

eat the skin   **do not eat the skin**

Which part of the diagram: red or green?

1 grapes   2 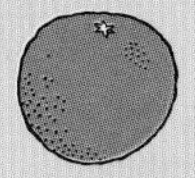   3 pineapple   4

5    6 pear   7    8 melon

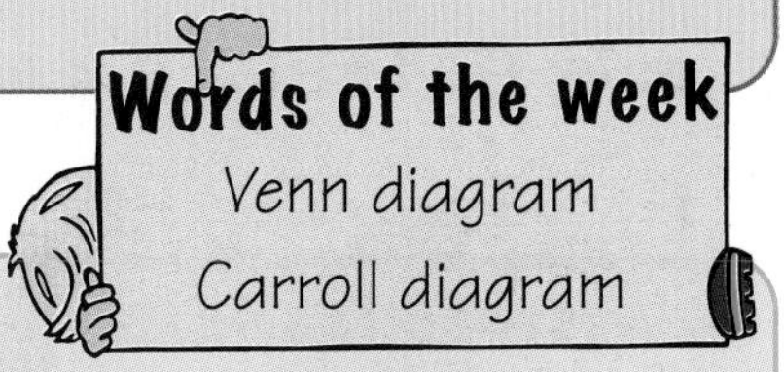

Words of the week
Venn diagram
Carroll diagram

Challenge

Draw three different diagrams for sorting a set of dominoes.

Review

0   500   1000

A Round each number to the nearest 100.

472   **350**   **549**   **385**   **835**

B 1   36   **2**   71   **3**   248   **4**   304
     + 48   – 36   + 69   – 56
    ____   ____   ____   ____

    ____   ____   ____   ____

C 1 1 litre = ☐ ml   **2** $\frac{1}{2}$ kg = ☐ g   **3** 1 km = ☐ m

D What is the time half an hour later?

1    2    3    4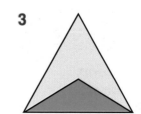

E Write the fraction that is coloured.

1   2   3   4

F **1** $5 \times \square = 45$ **2** $\square \times 10 = 70$ **3** $9 \times \square = 18$ **4** $\square \times 3 = 12$

G **1** $30 \div \square = 6$ **2** $24 \div \square = 8$ **3** $\square \div 10 = 8$ **4** $\square \div 2 = 8$

H Which of these are right angles?

1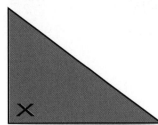

2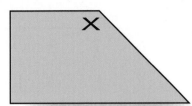

3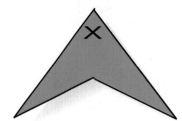

4

5

Which of the shapes are quadrilaterals?

I How much change from £10?

1  £4.70

2  £6.25

3  £7.75

4 £2.99

J What could the missing numbers be?

$\square \div \square = 3$ remainder 2

Number bonds

+	0	1	2	3	4	5	6	7	8	9	10
0	0	1	2	3	4	5	6	7	8	9	10
1	1	2	3	4	5	6	7	8	9	10	11
2	2	3	4	5	6	7	8	9	10	11	12
3	3	4	5	6	7	8	9	10	11	12	13
4	4	5	6	7	8	9	10	11	12	13	14
5	5	6	7	8	9	10	11	12	13	14	15
6	6	7	8	9	10	11	12	13	14	15	16
7	7	8	9	10	11	12	13	14	15	16	17
8	8	9	10	11	12	13	14	15	16	17	18
9	9	10	11	12	13	14	15	16	17	18	19
10	10	11	12	13	14	15	16	17	18	19	20

×	0	1	2	3	4	5	6	7	8	9	10
0	0	0	0	0	0	0	0	0	0	0	0
1	0	1	2	3	4	5	6	7	8	9	10
2	0	2	4	6	8	10	12	14	16	18	20
3	0	3	6	9	12	15	18	21	24	27	30
4	0	4	8	12	16	20	24	28	32	36	40
5	0	5	10	15	20	25	30	35	40	45	50

You should know these by heart.

Shapes

Name	sides	examples
triangle	3	
quadrilateral	4	
pentagon	5	
hexagon	6	
octagon	8	

Name	example
cube	
cuboid	
pyramid	
sphere	
hemisphere	
cone	
cylinder	
prism	

Angles and direction

turning clockwise   turning anticlockwise

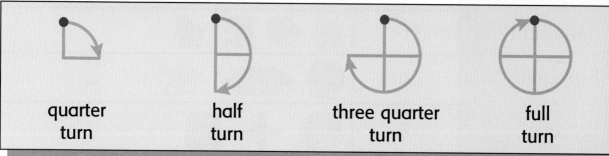

quarter turn   half turn   three quarter turn   full turn

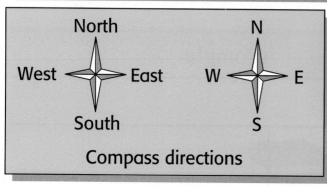

North   N

West   East   W   E

South   S

Compass directions

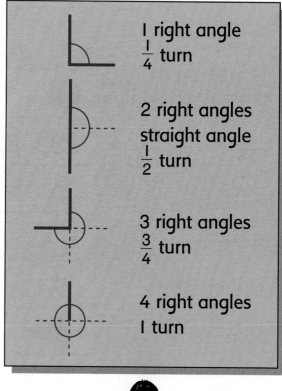

I right angle $\frac{1}{4}$ turn

2 right angles straight angle $\frac{1}{2}$ turn

3 right angles $\frac{3}{4}$ turn

4 right angles I turn

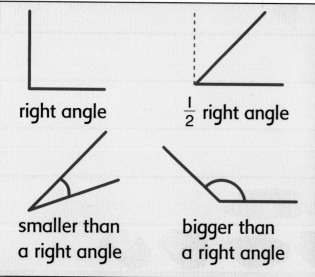

right angle $\frac{1}{2}$ right angle

smaller than a right angle   bigger than a right angle

left   right

Time and measures

Analogue time

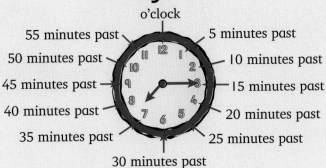

- 55 minutes past
- 50 minutes past
- 45 minutes past
- 40 minutes past
- 35 minutes past
- 30 minutes past
- o'clock
- 5 minutes past
- 10 minutes past
- 15 minutes past
- 20 minutes past
- 25 minutes past

seven fifteen (7.15) or 15 minutes past 7
- The small hand shows the hour.
- The longer hand shows how many minutes past the hour.

Digital time

shows the hour

shows how many minutes past

four thirty (4.30) or 30 minutes past 4

Monday
Tuesday
Wednesday
Thursday
Friday
Saturday
Sunday

---

1 minute   = 60 seconds

1 hour   = 60 minutes

1 day   = 24 hours

1 week   = 7 days

1 year   = 12 months

1 year   = 365 days

1 leap year = 366 days

1 century   = 100 years

---

month	days
January	31
February	28 (29 in a leap year)
March	31
April	30
May	31
June	30
July	31
August	31
September	30
October	31
November	30
December	31

---

1 centimetre = 10 millimetres

1 cm = 10 mm

1 metre = 100 centimetres

1 m = 100 cm

1 kilometre = 1000 metres

1 km = 1000 m

---

1 kilogram = 1000 grams

1 kg = 1000 g

1 litre = 1000 millilitres

1 l = 1000 ml

Do you remember?

Term 1 (pp. 4–5)

1b	2a	3b	4c	5c
6b	7a	8a	9c	10a

Term 2 (pp. 34–35)

1b	2b	3c	4c	5a
6a	7b	8a	9a	10c

Term 3 (pp. 62–63)

1c	2b	3b	4b	5c
6b	7b	8b	9a	10b.